Praise for *The Magic of Mindful Self-Awareness* and Matt Tenney's work

"*The Magic of Mindful Self-Awareness* draws you in with a powerful, inspiring story and provides you with a simple, practical path to dramatically reducing negative thoughts and emotions and realizing more positivity, happiness, and meaning in your life. I'm looking forward to seeing how this book changes lives."

—**Jon Gordon, best-selling author of** *The Energy Bus,* *The One Truth,* **and** *The Power of Positive Leadership*

"Matt Tenney has a clarity about the world that is remarkable. His experience and the lessons he learned need to be heard by as many people as possible."

—**Simon Sinek, NYT best-selling author of** *Start with Why* **and** *Leaders Eat Last*

"In *The Magic of Mindful Self-Awareness*, Matt Tenney provides compelling evidence that it's possible to be happy for no reason, regardless of your situation in life. This engaging book includes Matt's remarkable story of discovering happiness while in solitary confinement. You'll find both inspiration and a powerful, practical path to building lasting habits for happiness and fulfillment."

—**Marci Shimoff, #1 NYT best-selling author of** *Happy for No Reason*

"This is one of those rare books you just can't put down. *The Magic of Mindful Self-Awareness* combines an extraordinary story with life-changing insights that challenge much conventional thinking. I recommend this book to anyone who wants to be happier or more effective because it will help you with both."

—**John Spence, author of *Awesomely Simple* and named one of the top 100 business thought leaders in America by Trust Across America**

"Imagine for a moment that the happiness, meaning, and fulfillment you have passionately been searching for has been hiding in plain sight all along—utterly available—in the palm of your hand. Now imagine that you are introduced to such wisdom directly, during the most challenging moment of your life. Matt Tenney didn't have to imagine such things. He lived them: intimately, fearlessly, and nobly. In *The Magic of Mindful Self-Awareness*, Matt shares his journey along with practical guidance for helping you discover the happiness, meaning, and fulfillment that is closer to you than you might think."

—**Michael Carroll, author of *Awake at Work* and *The Mindful Leader***

"I've studied mindfulness with Ivy League professors, completed intensive meditation programs, and nothing stuck—until I read *The Magic of Mindful Self-Awareness*. In just days, I experienced real transformation. Matt Tenney's approach is simple, powerful, and *finally* something that works in real life."

—**Jill Schulman, Former USMC officer, keynote speaker, and author and researcher on the science of bravery**

Also by Matt Tenney

Inspire Greatness: How to Motivate Employees with a Simple, Repeatable, Scalable Process

The Mindfulness Edge: How to Rewire Your Brain for Leadership and Personal Excellence Without Adding to Your Schedule

Serve to Be Great: Leadership Lessons from a Prison, a Monastery, and a Boardroom

The Magic of Mindful Self-Awareness

How to Stop Overthinking, Clear Your Mind, and Be Happy (Almost) All the Time

Matt Tenney

The Magic of Mindful Self-Awareness © 2025 by Matt Tenney

All rights reserved. No part of this book may be sold or reproduced in any form without written permission from the publisher, except for brief quotations embodied in critical articles or reviews.

Published by
PeopleThriver LLC
7051 HWY 70 S, Suite 136
Nashville, TN 37221
www.PeopleThriver.com

First printing edition in the United States of America 2025

ISBN 979-8-218-57892-3

Cover design by Distinguish 99Designs
Edited by Leah Acosta
Copy Editing and Proofreading by Muriel Call, Grisel Marsh, and Emma Moylan

Although the publisher and the author have made every effort to ensure that the information in this book was correct at press time and while this publication is designed to provide accurate information in regard to the subject matter covered, the publisher and the author assume no responsibility for errors, inaccuracies, omissions, or any other inconsistencies herein and hereby disclaim any liability to any party for any loss, damage, or disruption caused by errors or omissions, whether such errors or omissions result from negligence, accident, or any other cause. The ideas in this book are the opinions of the author expressed in good faith and not meant to be professional medical or mental health advice. Before making any decision regarding courses of action that could affect your mental or physical health, you should consult a licensed professional. Neither the author nor the publisher makes any guarantees regarding any outcome that may or may not result from the ideas contained in this book.

*This book is dedicated to you, the reader.
May it help you to realize unconditional happiness and bring greater
happiness to others.*

Contents

Part One

How I Discovered Unconditional Happiness on My Journey from Prisoner to Monk to Social Entrepreneur

1. The Failure That Almost Cost Me My Life — 13
2. Finding Happiness and Meaning in One of the Most Stressful Places in the World — 17
3. From Selfish Neurotic to Happy Servant: Why I Wrote This Book and How It Could Change Your Life — 24

Part Two

How to Stop Overthinking, Clear Your Mind, and Be Happy 95% of the Time

4. How to Be Free from Your Thoughts So You Can Stop Overthinking and Enjoy the Present Moment — 35
5. How to Clear Your Mind and Make the Practice of Mindful Self-Awareness (Almost) Effortless — 45
6. The Life-Changing Habit of Taking the Ultimate Vacation Every Day Before Bedtime — 53
7. An Extraordinary Paradigm Shift: How to Transform Mundane Activities Into Magical Moments and Be Happy 95% of the Time — 60

Part Three
Awakening to Your True Self: How to Be at Peace During the 5% of Life That Is Truly Painful and Live a Deeply Meaningful Life

8. The Wisdom That Frees You from All Suffering: Realizing Your True Self	73
9. How to Be Free from Panic Attacks, Anxiety, and Other Unpleasant Emotions	91
10. A Simple Path to Living a Deeply Meaningful Life	104
Acknowledgments	117
About the Author	119
Notes	121

Part One

How I Discovered Unconditional Happiness on My Journey from Prisoner to Monk to Social Entrepreneur

Chapter 1
The Failure That Almost Cost Me My Life

In the fall of the year 2000, the proverbial "perfect storm" was brewing in the mundane drama that was my life.

From the outside, my life looked just fine. I was proudly serving as an officer in the United States Marine Corps. I was making what I thought was a good living. I was madly in love with my fun and gorgeous girlfriend from Brazil whom I was considering marrying. I also had plenty of time to pursue my interests, like Brazilian jiujitsu and fitness.

However, on the inside, I was a mess. I spent most of my free time dwelling on what was wrong in my life.

Since I was on deployment at the time, I was unable to spend time with my girlfriend. I worried about a financial issue that resulted from selling my condo with owner financing to a person who stopped making loan payments to me. And, I had a nagging stress fracture that prevented me from running, which was my go-to outlet for stress relief.

As I had done most of my life, I looked to the future for happiness. I thought continuously about how much happier I would be once I returned from deployment, was reunited with my girlfriend, finished my time in the Marine Corps, resolved the financial issue with the person who stopped paying me what he owed, and started working toward financial freedom.

Although I had dealt with anxiety and bouts of depression on and off throughout my life, I had never experienced anything like what I experienced while on deployment. I worried almost all the time and, as a result, exhausted myself, resulting in the deepest sense of depression I had ever experienced.

Unaware that I was creating, with my thinking, most of the anxiety and depression I experienced, I continued spending nearly all my time dwelling on what was wrong and on how much better things would be in the future.

It was during this time of significant depression that I had the conversation that would change the course of my life in ways I never could have imagined.

I was chatting with a friend of mine, who was a disbursing officer. We were talking about our jobs, and he casually mentioned how easy it was for him to procure the $4.5 million in cash we had on the ship. We joked about what a great story it would make if someone "ran off into the sunset with a few million dollars."

Not long after that conversation, as a way to distract myself from my constant unwanted thinking, I started working on an outline for a novel based on the ideas that my friend and I joked about. I had several more conversations with him and asked him about the details of how he procured the money.

It wasn't long before I had what I needed to write a very realistic novel. In fact, I thought, I probably knew enough to actually arrange a delivery of funds in real life.

At first, I didn't seriously consider ever doing anything with the information I had obtained other than potentially writing the novel about it.

However, after I returned home from deployment and began the discharge process from the Marine Corps, my dream of starting my civilian life with my girlfriend was shattered. She told me that she was no longer in love with me and she wanted to end our relationship.

After the shock wore off, I sank into an even deeper depression than what I had experienced while on deployment. I told myself, *You have*

The Magic of Mindful Self-Awareness

nothing to lose anymore. Why not see if you can at least arrange the delivery of a few million dollars and then decide if you want to actually go through with taking it? This could potentially solve all of your problems and finally allow you to be happy.

I also told myself, *This would be a victimless crime. The government wastes billions of dollars every year. They would just write off a loss of only a few million dollars and print more money.*

I somehow convinced myself to believe this self-talk and, in January 2001, I took several steps to arrange the unauthorized delivery of $2.9 million.

Then, after I had arranged the delivery, reality hit me.

I felt horrible for being dishonest and I realized that there was no way I could go through with it. I did not want to be a criminal. I didn't even have a plan for picking up the money. I decided to abandon the whole idea and head to Brazil, with the few thousand dollars I had in the bank, to start a new life.

I didn't make it.

While I was en route to the airport, I was pulled over, physically removed from my Jeep at gunpoint, and arrested by agents of the Federal Bureau of Investigation (FBI).

After being interrogated by FBI agents and admitting everything I had done, I was taken to a federal detention center in San Diego, California. But it wasn't long before the US military took jurisdiction of my case.

Although I was no longer going to work each day for the Marine Corps, I had not received my final discharge papers yet. I was still technically employed by the US military. Thus, after the military took jurisdiction of my case, I was transferred to the base brig—a military prison—at Camp Pendleton in California.

Because I was an officer, I was not allowed to interact with enlisted Marines and was required to spend about twenty-two hours per day alone in a six-foot-by-nine-foot prison cell. I was essentially in solitary confinement.

This gave me plenty of time to think about how stupid I had been. I thought almost constantly about how angry I was at myself.

I thought about how this was definitely not a victimless crime, as I had told myself before. I caused a lot of suffering for my family, friends, and fellow Marines, which I deeply regretted, and still regret today.

I thought about how by doing several dishonest things, I had deviated almost unrecognizably from my character up to that point. I thought about how hard it would be to earn back people's trust. I thought I would probably never have a normal life.

The peak of my suffering occurred not long after arriving at the brig.

Although I did not attempt to take possession of government money, the steps I took to arrange the unauthorized delivery made me guilty of attempted fraud. My lawyers told me that in the federal system, according to the federal sentencing guidelines, my actions would have likely resulted in me being sentenced to about eighteen months of confinement in a minimum-security camp with no fences. However, the military court was not required to follow the federal sentencing guidelines.

I'll never forget the first time I spoke with my military lawyer. We were looking at each other through the food tray slot in the cell door. The slot measured about three inches high and twelve inches wide. I asked him how long I might spend in the brig.

He had almost no expression on his face as he looked at me with his piercing blue eyes. He told me that, based on all of the charges I was facing, the maximum possible sentence was eighty-five years. He said it was possible that I could spend seventy to eighty years in the brig.

I went into shock. I don't remember much about the next day or so.

I do remember that for several weeks after that conversation, I had suicidal thoughts flashing through my mind almost continuously. During that time, every night when I went to bed, I prayed that I wouldn't wake up in the morning.

Chapter 2
Finding Happiness and Meaning in One of the Most Stressful Places in the World

As you've probably guessed, my prayers went unanswered. I kept waking up in the morning.

I was eventually found guilty of attempted fraud at a court-martial. Since I had admitted to authorities everything I had done and agreed to plead guilty, the government offered me a pretrial agreement to save time and expense. The agreement capped my time in confinement to eight years. As long as I followed the rules while confined, this meant I would spend about six years in prison.

I was twenty-four years old at the time, so six years still sounded like a very long time. But it was clearly better than eighty years and I was soon able to come to terms with the fate I had created for myself.

Although I was still in what amounted to solitary confinement, I started to adjust and I began to look for what opportunities might be found in my situation. After all, I had a lot of time on my hands.

I spent a lot of time reading and learning about a variety of topics and eventually asked the most powerful two questions I know of for transforming an unpleasant situation into one that can be deeply meaningful. Those questions are:

What can I learn from this?
How will this help me to better serve others?

Asking those questions led to a deeper exploration of spirituality. It was during this time of exploring spirituality that an interesting question came to me. I wondered, *Is it possible to be just as happy in a prison cell as I could be after I was released?*

I had read about monks from various spiritual traditions who voluntarily chose to live in circumstances very similar to the one I was in. Of course, most monks aren't confined to a cell for twenty-two hours per day, or constantly humiliated by prison guards, or concerned about the threat of violence from other inmates. However, just like my experience in prison, they have almost no possessions and are not able to enjoy most of the things laypeople enjoy every day.

I decided that since many wise spiritual teachers actively encourage monks to live simply to accelerate their spiritual development, it must be possible to be just as happy in a prison cell as I could be after I was free.

I asked my mother to send me a few books written by monks on how to train the mind to be happy. In one of the books she sent, a monk mentioned a simple idea that I had never considered before: comparative thinking—comparing the present moment to the past or future—is a significant cause of dissatisfaction.

This idea really caught my attention, so I took some time to contemplate it. The results of that contemplation would change the course of my life once again.

I realized that, assuming I am not experiencing significant physical pain, if I'm not comparing my experience in the present moment to memories of experiences I've had in the past, or to thoughts of experiences I could have in the future, there's nothing wrong with the experience I am having right now.

The present-moment experience is just fine. In fact, it's actually perfect.

As I took time to further contemplate this insight, a path to true freedom became clear.

It occurred to me that if I could be free from comparative thinking while I was getting dressed in the morning, that moment would be perfect. If I could then be free from comparative thinking while brushing my teeth, that moment would be perfect. If I could then be

The Magic of Mindful Self-Awareness

free from comparative thinking while eating breakfast, that moment would be perfect.

If I could gradually learn to be free from comparative thinking during each waking moment, each moment would be just fine, even in prison. In fact, I could realize the inherent perfection of each moment.

I saw the distinct possibility that I could be free right where I was, because the real prison was not my prison cell. The real prison was my own mind.

I realized that this true freedom does not depend on being physically free or financially free. In fact, it doesn't depend on anything outside of ourselves. It is trainable.

In case this sounds like nothing more than wishful thinking, or that it's something that you don't think could be possible for you, I'd like to point out that you've already experienced many months of your life realizing the perfection of the present-moment experience.

If you observe babies, you'll notice that, unless they truly need something because they are scared, overtired, hungry, or experiencing physical discomfort (like a dirty diaper), babies are perfectly happy in each and every moment.

Lay babies on the floor doing nothing and they're perfectly happy. Put them in a car that's stuck in a traffic jam and they're perfectly happy. Put them in a stroller with no view of anything in particular and they're perfectly happy.

Babies don't need anything to entertain them. They don't need to have particular possessions. They don't need fine foods or drinks. Just to be alive in any average moment is enough.

You, like other babies, experienced this sort of heaven on earth for many months before your mind started developing the habit of identifying with comparative thoughts, which led you to being increasingly less satisfied with "ordinary" moments.

After spending a day or so joyfully contemplating the possibility of being just as happy in prison as I could be anywhere else, I began to practice *mindful self-awareness*, which is the most important aspect of the well-known practice of mindfulness.[1]

Mindful self-awareness allows us to be aware of thoughts instead of being identified with them. As soon as I started practicing this, I noticed that in any moment I could see my thoughts as objects of awareness, those thoughts just came and went. They no longer distracted me from the inherent perfection of the present-moment experience.

Little by little, over a period of months, the practice of mindful self-awareness began to permeate nearly every waking moment of each day. About six months after beginning the practice, I noticed something that seemed very strange to me at first: I was thriving in one of the most stressful environments in the world.

In fact, I was happier in prison—with no possessions, no entertainment, and no romantic relationships—than I had ever been in my life.

I realized through direct experience that happiness does not depend on any external condition being met. We can train our minds to be happy no matter what circumstances we encounter in life. This is the magic of mindful self-awareness.

This realization of unconditional happiness inspired me to go as deep as I could with the practice, not just for my own benefit, but for the benefit of others. I knew that the better I understood how the mind works and how to be free from the prison of the mind, the more helpful I could be to others who would also like to be free from their thinking.

I had been learning about how to train the mind principally from the written teachings of Catholic monks, Zen monks, Tibetan monks, and Theravadan monks. The more I learned about monastic training, the more it appealed to me.

After being released from the form of solitary confinement I had been in and moved into the general population of the prison, I decided that I would not use the relative freedom I was given to entertain and distract myself from the experience of being confined. Instead, I decided to treat the prison as though it were a monastery, to become a novice monk, and to spend the remaining four years of confinement living and training exactly as monks live and train.

I didn't read any novels and watched almost no television or movies. I tried to speak very little and to do much more listening. I trained my mind with the practice of mindful self-awareness while sitting still for several hours each day and during nearly every other waking moment of the day.

It's possible you might think of monks as being lazy people who spend all day contemplating their navels (or something equally worthless) and who don't contribute much to society. I actually used to have similar thoughts about monks. However, I came to realize that the monastic path is a very meaningful one that brings great benefit to others.

The core of monastic training is to train one's own mind to be happy, so that we can better help others to be happy, and to cultivate the most important qualities of being human, like kindness, compassion, and generosity. This allows us to make a positive impact in the lives of others with each interaction. To have the best chance of achieving these goals, monks give up all short-term, selfish desires and live as simply as possible, devoting all their energy to training the mind.

The monastic path is one that is completely devoted to the service of others. Living this way transformed my experience of being confined to prison into the most meaningful experience of my life because it allowed me to help others every single day.

It's apparently not normal for a person to walk around prison happy all the time. As a result, I was asked on almost a daily basis some variation of the question, "Dude, what type of drugs are they giving you?"

When I responded that I wasn't taking any medication (or consuming any type of intoxicants), I was eventually almost always asked, "How can you be so happy in this place?"

This opened the door to many conversations about how it's possible to train the mind to be happy and about practical steps for beginning that training.

I realized that if I could help an inmate to be free from suffering, it would be a gift to both him and anyone he interacts with. And, it would significantly reduce the chances that he would commit another crime after being released.

I realized that if I could help a guard to be free from suffering, he would be more likely to be kind to his friends, neighbors, and wife. Those people would then be a little kinder to others, and so on.

I could see how, through a ripple effect, I was having a positive impact on society right there from the inside of the prison. This further energized me and deepened my inspiration to practice.

As a result of practicing more and more intensively, there were also several profound experiences of spiritual awakening, which I'll describe more in chapter 8. These experiences helped me to discover my true self, the part of us that is always at peace. I eventually also discovered how the practice of mindful self-awareness allows us to be our true selves whenever we'd like to be, and how spending more time being our true selves transforms us into happier, kinder, and more compassionate people.

After a few years of practice, I found my time in confinement to be so meaningful that I would not have been upset at all if I had been told that I would have to spend the rest of my life there. I was fully prepared to continue practicing and serving others from inside the prison if that's what was meant to be.

As it turned out, it was not meant to be.

After five and a half years of living, practicing, and serving inside a prison, I was released. However, serving others—principally by training to be happy, kind, compassionate, and generous—has been my main focus in life ever since. I envision a world in which poverty, violence, and other unnecessary suffering no longer exist. Since leaving confinement, nearly everything I've done has been in furtherance of making this vision a reality.

The Magic of Mindful Self-Awareness

Key Ideas from Chapter 2

1. A powerful practice for turning unpleasant situations into opportunities for meaning and fulfillment is to ask the following two questions:
    - *What can I learn from this?*
    - *How will this help me to better serve others?*
2. Happiness doesn't depend on circumstances in life. Happiness is trainable with the practice of mindful self-awareness.

Chapter 3
From Selfish Neurotic to Happy Servant: Why I Wrote This Book and How It Could Change Your Life

Since I had just spent nearly four years living and training as a monk, when I first left confinement, I thought the most natural path of service was to be formally ordained as a monk. Accordingly, I went to live in a monastery for a few months and was almost ordained to be a monk for the rest of my life.

Ultimately, though, I realized that if I wanted to best grow my ability to be of service to others, I needed to continue practicing with the same dedication but do so out in the so-called "real world." I needed to earn a living, pay bills, navigate relationships, and deal with all of the other challenges that most people face on a daily basis.

After deciding not to be ordained, I began looking for ways I could serve. First, I went to live in Mazatlán, a city in western Mexico, where I did volunteer work with underprivileged children.

When I returned to the United States, I moved to Gainesville, Florida, and started a nonprofit organization called the True Freedom Foundation, which had two main programs.

First, I self-published a book called *A Practical Guide to True Happiness and Freedom*, which we sent to inmates for free to help them heal while in confinement and potentially find true happiness like I did.

Second, we offered the Ultimate Warrior Program in partnership

The Magic of Mindful Self-Awareness

with the police department in Gainesville. We worked to help prevent underprivileged youth from ending up in the criminal justice system. Through the program, young people learned how to train their minds to develop self-awareness and self-control as part of mixed martial arts training that focused heavily on Brazilian jiujitsu.

The core idea of the Ultimate Warrior Program was that the ultimate warrior is not the one who masters the fists. The ultimate warrior is the one who masters the mind.

While running the True Freedom Foundation, I was asked to cofound and be the initial instructor for the Florida chapter of a now international nonprofit organization called Kids Kicking Cancer. Since I was unable to secure enough funding to keep the True Freedom Foundation going, I decided to wind down that work and shift my attention toward Kids Kicking Cancer.

I quickly discovered incredible meaning and fulfillment in my new role. Kids Kicking Cancer team members work with amazing young heroes who are dealing with very serious diagnoses like sickle cell anemia, cystic fibrosis, and cancer.

Through the training they receive, children learn that they can lower their own pain levels by "tapping into their own inner power" using the "secrets of the martial arts." The tools include breath work and mindful self-awareness training, which have a large body of evidence supporting their efficacy for regulating emotion and pain.

I've personally worked with young heroes who, after receiving some training, could lower their own pain levels, in a matter of minutes, from a nine-out-of-ten on a pain scale down to a two, or a one, or sometimes even a zero. In some cases, we didn't even need to be in the room with them. They could achieve those types of results entirely on their own, which was incredibly empowering for them.

Within a few months, I was asked to be the director of the Kids Kicking Cancer program in Florida. I worked to bring on volunteers, hire staff, and build a local board of directors.

While I was working as a director with Kids Kicking Cancer, I was asked to start providing mindful self-awareness training for nurses. This led to requests to conduct training for other professionals and leaders. One engagement led to another, then others.

Soon, I was delivering numerous leadership training programs and keynote speeches at leadership meetings and conferences. These programs help leaders to see the value of working to better serve their employees. They also help leaders use mindful self-awareness training to increase their capacity to bring out the best in team members, while also realizing greater happiness and fulfillment in their work as leaders.

My professional focus began shifting to helping leaders better serve employees. As much as I loved working directly with young heroes in the hospital and running the Kids Kicking Cancer program in Florida, I thought I could make an even bigger impact in our world by helping leaders help employees to better thrive. I reasoned that each time I help a senior leader in a large organization, I can make a positive impact on the lives of hundreds or even thousands of employees.

Life started to move very quickly.

I met a wonderful woman named Leah who embodies an amazing combination of thoughtfulness, creativity, and intelligence. She is a true Renaissance woman. We grew our friendship for several months, then began courting. After getting the Kids Kicking Cancer program in Florida to the point where it would run just as well, or better, without me, I proposed to Leah and followed her to Nashville, Tennessee.

In the same year Leah and I were married (2014), I published my first leadership book, called *Serve to Be Great*, with one of the largest publishing companies in the world, Wiley. I got even busier, and was soon traveling about fifty times a year to deliver inspirational leadership keynote speeches and training programs on leadership and mindful self-awareness.

In 2015, our first child was born. I decided to do less traveling so I could be more present as a father. I wrote and published my second leadership book with Wiley, called *The Mindfulness Edge*, but I accepted fewer and fewer speaking engagements.

I decided to start a second business, a marketing company called The Generous Group, that wouldn't require so much travel. More importantly, my goal was to build what I hoped would be the best workplace culture in the world: a workplace that had a positive impact on the physical, mental, and spiritual well-being of all employees. I believe that creating workplaces like this is one of the keys to realizing my vision of a world in which poverty, violence, and other unnecessary suffering no longer exist.

I decided on a marketing company because I hoped that building a team with expertise in marketing would one day allow me to scale the impact I'm trying to make in our world through leadership development and improving workplace cultures.

The company is a social enterprise because I am what's known as a *social entrepreneur*. I'm not interested in accumulating wealth or possessions. I see profit as "impact fuel," which we use to benefit our team members and society as a whole, instead of enriching the owners of the company.

After spending a few years growing The Generous Group, I finally "connected the dots" on how we could combine all that my team and I had learned about start-ups, marketing, and leadership development to scale our efforts to help leaders, and the employees they serve, to better thrive.

I cofounded another social enterprise, called PeopleThriver, which offers a groundbreaking approach to employee engagement and leadership development that is automated with the use of software. I believe that the work we do to create sustainable, high-performance workplace cultures where people can truly thrive is the fastest way to realize our vision of a world in which poverty, violence, and other unnecessary suffering no longer exist.

Our approach to employee engagement and leadership development is so effective that I decided to write my third leadership book, called *Inspire Greatness*, as a way to share the approach with as many leaders as possible. Thanks to what my team and I had learned about marketing over the years, we were able to launch *Inspire Greatness* in May of 2024 as a USA Today, LA Times, and Publishers Weekly bestseller.

Why I Wrote This Book

One morning, about six months after the release of *Inspire Greatness*, I was sitting still, practicing mindful self-awareness, and I felt a tremendous amount of suffering. It wasn't coming from me. It was something I could sense coming from millions of people in the United States.

I had been aware that mental health in the US, on average, has been declining for the last ten years, particularly among young people. Americans have been reporting increasing levels of stress, worry, depression, and anger for years. In fact, earlier this year, 2024, the US hit a ten-year low in its world happiness ranking in the World Happiness Report.

But this particular morning I could literally *feel* the suffering of millions of Americans. It was close to Election Day and our country seemed to be more divided than it has been at any time since the Civil War. I felt very intense levels of both anger and sadness coming from people all over the country.

I'm not sure why, but I then felt a tremendous sense of empathy for everyone, regardless of their political views. I could see and understand why both liberals and conservatives felt the way they did. I could also see why it's become so hard for liberals and conservatives to listen to and understand each other.

I allowed the suffering to be experienced deeply for a few minutes. Then I applied the practice of mindful self-awareness to allow the emotions and all associated thoughts to dissipate.

Then, a strong sense of compassion arose. I just wanted people to be happier and kinder to each other. This compassion gave rise to joy. I sat with a clear mind for another few minutes, enjoying the compassion and joy I felt, before the timer on my phone sounded, which signaled the end of my sitting still practice.

When I got up to start the rest of the morning routine, I had several deeply moving thoughts.

I thought about how, after a lifetime of suffering from anxiety and depression, I no longer suffer from either. In the last ten years or so I have only experienced anxiety or sadness a few times, for a few brief seconds each time. I thought about how much I'd like to help everyone in our country, as well as everyone else around the world, to experience the same freedom I experience so they suffer much less, are more consistently happy, and are more consistently kind to each other.

Writing a book seemed like the most likely way to accomplish this.

But I immediately began doubting that I could reach millions of people with a book. I had shared similar ideas in *A Practical Guide to True Happiness and Freedom,* *Serve to Be Great,* and *The Mindfulness*

The Magic of Mindful Self-Awareness

Edge. Although many people told me those books were among the best books they had ever read on the topic, and the two published by Wiley did well compared to most books, none of those books were bestsellers.

Then, I had a bit of an epiphany.

I've since learned that it takes more than writing a good book to reach millions of people. I've learned that a book won't usually start selling itself until thirty thousand to fifty thousand people in one country have read it in a period of a year or so. And, even then, most books require continued investment to reach millions of people.

When I wrote my first three books, I didn't know much about book marketing, I didn't have much capital to invest in launching and continuing to market the books, and I didn't have much of a personal or professional network to help get the books off the ground.

I realized that none of those barriers exist now. Thanks to the success of The Generous Group and PeopleThriver, my team and I know a lot about book marketing (which allowed us to launch *Inspire Greatness* as a national bestseller), we have sufficient capital to invest in launching and continuing to market this book, and my network has grown substantially.

I became very confident that I could ensure this book would be read by at least fifty thousand people in the first year or so.

Also, because readers told me that the earlier books were excellent—and since then I have learned even more about how to help others with the practice of mindful self-awareness—I was very confident that I could make this book an absolutely life-changing guide that could make a significant, positive impact on anyone who reads it.

As these thoughts came to me, I became so excited that I started planning and writing this book immediately, despite how busy I am leading two small companies and raising two young children. I devoted every moment I could to this book without compromising my other commitments.

I still believe that helping leaders make a more consistently positive impact on the lives of employees is the most highly leveraged way to make a positive impact on society. However, I want to help people thrive with both a top-down approach and this more direct approach, and I'm now very confident that this book will quickly and directly help millions of people to be happier.

My goal is to ensure that this book is read by at least one million people in the next five years.

Also, there are several insights I'd like to share that I've never shared in any book before. These insights will help you avoid the years of struggle that I experienced with the practice of mindful self-awareness and make the practice almost effortless for you.

There is no personal profit motive for this book. Accordingly, although I'm certainly not opposed to earning a living from writing books, and I am compensated for some other books, I will never be personally compensated from the sales of *this* book.

In fact, I plan to invest around $50,000 to launch this book and ensure that at least fifty thousand people read it in the first year. All proceeds that exceed what it costs to ensure the book reaches fifty thousand people in the first year will be invested in either reaching the goal of ensuring one million people read this book in the next five years or in other projects that help people to better thrive.

How This Book Could Change Your Life

In the pages that follow, you'll learn a simple, logical, step-by-step path for training your mind for unconditional happiness without adding anything to your schedule.

Following are some of the specific things you'll learn:

- How to stop overthinking with a simple, effortless life hack
- How to clear your mind of unwanted thoughts
- How to improve your creativity and clarity of thought
- How to be happy during any moment that isn't painful and be at peace during even the most painful moments of life
- How to stop anxiety attacks and panic attacks more quickly
- How to transform unpleasant emotions like sadness and anger into compassion and joy
- How to improve productivity by taking the ultimate

The Magic of Mindful Self-Awareness

vacation, whenever you want to, without going anywhere or spending any money
- How to discover your true self—the part of you that is always at peace—and cultivate the wisdom that sets you free from all suffering
- How to live a meaningful life that makes a significant, positive impact on others
- How to form lasting, life-changing habits that positively impact every aspect of your life

Perhaps most exciting for you is that you won't have to live and train like a monk for years, as I did, to realize the benefits listed above. Over the last two decades of practicing and teaching—which includes over ten thousand hours of formal sitting still practice and many more hours of practicing mindful self-awareness during daily activities—I have personally helped thousands of people to be happier, less stressed, and more effective. I am very confident that I'll be able to help you advance in the practice very quickly and discover the magic of mindful self-awareness for yourself.

However, I hesitate to state that I'll be "teaching you" things. I'll be more like a guide who helps you discover life-changing truths for yourself. Any benefits you realize will not be the result of reading this book. The benefits will be the result of the actions you take, the habits you develop, and the insights that you discover while practicing mindful self-awareness.

This is why I include action steps at the end of every chapter from now on. I want to make it as easy as possible for you to take action and to build and maintain the life-changing habits you'll learn in this book.

I am extremely confident that if you read the remainder of this book and take action on what you learn, the actions you take and the habits you build will change your life in ways that you may have never imagined. Also, as you become more consistently free from suffering and consistently happier, you'll make a significant, positive impact on everyone you encounter.

In fact, you might just change the world.

Key Ideas from Chapter 3

1. There is a simple, logical, step-by-step path that will allow you to stop overthinking, clear your mind, and be happy (almost) all the time. You will learn that path in this book.
2. In order to realize the many benefits of mindful self-awareness, you'll need to take action on what you learn in this book. I'll make it easy for you by offering action steps and free resources on MattTenney.com to help you.

Action Steps for Chapter 3

1. Please download and print the free *The Magic of Mindful Self-Awareness Practice Tracker* available at MattTenney.com and write out your goals and commitment on the form per the following action steps.
2. Please take a moment to write out the most important one to three changes you'd like to see in your life as a result of reading this book.
3. Please write out a commitment to yourself to apply what you learn in this book to realize the changes you wrote above.

Part Two

How to Stop Overthinking, Clear Your Mind, and Be Happy 95% of the Time

Chapter 4
How to Be Free from Your Thoughts So You Can Stop Overthinking and Enjoy the Present Moment

I'll never forget the day I realized, beyond just the conceptual level, why the practice of mindful self-awareness is truly magic. It was a little over two years into my time in confinement.

I was in my prison cell, brushing my teeth and experiencing a profound sense of peace and joy. About halfway through brushing my teeth, I saw myself in the shiny piece of steel on the wall, which served as a mirror, above the steel sink.

I was reminded that I was definitely *physically* located in a prison. But I just observed the thought with mindful self-awareness. The thought vanished and my mind was empty of thinking once again.

Then, as I allowed the joy I felt to permeate my entire being, I thought, *If I'm just brushing my teeth, how is brushing my teeth in this prison cell any different from brushing my teeth in the last five-star hotel I stayed in or in a house I will return to one day in the future?*

The answer was clear. If I wasn't caught up in comparative thinking, or if the mind was empty of thought, then brushing teeth in a prison cell was no different than brushing teeth anywhere else. It's just brushing teeth.

This wasn't just a thought. It's hard to describe in words, but this was a deep insight into the truth that I could have been anywhere in the world at that moment. Perhaps, in a way, I was "anywhere," "everywhere," or "nowhere," all at the same time. No words seemed to capture the experience correctly. It was truly *just brushing teeth*.

Because I was practicing mindful self-awareness in the way you'll soon learn, free from thoughts and being truly curious about the experience of brushing my teeth, I experienced a joy comparable to some of the most joyful moments of my life. I experienced this joy despite the fact that I was in a prison cell doing nothing other than brushing my teeth.

Then, I transitioned to walking, still practicing mindful self-awareness. Although the joy faded a bit, I was still perfectly content to just simply walk. In fact, I was happy the rest of the day. I was no longer "in prison." I was just brushing teeth, just walking, just sitting, just eating, and so on. I was truly free.

Let's consider how this could have gone very differently. Let's imagine that while brushing my teeth, I saw myself in the "mirror" and I was reminded that I was physically located in a prison. What if, in that moment, instead of allowing that thought to arise and pass away, I identified with it?

The moment we identify with a thought, we get caught in it, and we start talking to ourselves, generating more thoughts. Identifying with a thought is what triggers overthinking. What would have almost certainly happened is that I would have told myself a story about how I was in a cell, inside a prison surrounded by barbed-wire fences, and that the prison was a stressful, boring place with almost none of the pleasures afforded to people outside of prison.

I probably would have reminded myself that there were guards who often demeaned inmates and that there was an almost constant potential for violence. I probably would have told myself that I would have to be in this terrible place for nearly four more years. I probably would have thought about how much better things would be once I was released from prison.

By getting caught up in these comparative thoughts, I would have likely experienced anxiety, sadness, and frustration.

Thanks to the magic of mindful self-awareness, I never identified with the thought *I am brushing my teeth in a prison cell*. The thought

The Magic of Mindful Self-Awareness

just came and went, so I was just brushing my teeth, then just walking, then just sitting, and so on. As a result, instead of anxiety, sadness, and frustration, I experienced *happiness*.

As you read this, it's possible that you just remembered a profound truth that you may have forgotten: the problems in our lives don't result from what happens to us but from what we think about what happens to us.

We create problems by talking to ourselves, overthinking, and telling ourselves negative stories about what happens to us.

There's an old story that makes this point very clear.

* * *

One day, a wise old farmer is working outside when his horses break the fence and run away.

A neighbor of the farmer comes over and says, "I'm sorry your horses ran away. That is so bad."

The wise old farmer replies, "Who can say what is good or bad?"

A few days later, the farmer's horses return to his farm. Along with them, there's a new horse as well.

The neighbor comes over once again and says, "I'm glad you've acquired a new horse. That is so good!"

The farmer once again replies, "Who can say what is good or bad?"

The next day, the farmer's son is out training the new horse when he falls off and breaks his leg.

The neighbor once again comes over and says, "I'm sorry your son broke his leg. That is so bad."

The farmer again replies, "Who can say what is good or bad?"

A week later, the army comes through the area, requiring all young men to enlist and go off to a very bloody war where many young men would likely die.

The soldiers do not require the farmer's son to enlist because of his broken leg.

The neighbor comes over once again and says, "I'm glad that your son won't have to go to war. That is so good!"

And, the farmer once again replies, "Who can say what is good or bad?"

* * *

The point of the story above lies in a question: Where does the story end?

Of course, the story never ends. There is ultimately no such thing as a "good" or "bad" experience. What happens to us only appears to be "good" or "bad" based on what happens next. What we initially think of as being the worst thing that ever happened to us may one day be thought of as something that had an overall positive impact on us.

When I was initially confined to prison, I thought it was the worst thing that ever happened in my life. Looking back now, though, I see my time in confinement as the best thing that ever happened to me.

Of course, I deeply regret the suffering I caused for my peers, my friends, and my family as a result of the poor decisions I made. However, if I could go back in time and decide whether or not to relive the confinement experience all over again, as long as I wouldn't cause suffering for others, I would do it, without a moment of hesitation.

How to Be Free from Thoughts with the Practice of Mindful Self-Awareness

One might be tempted to think that if we just told ourselves better stories, we could solve all of our problems. While this is somewhat true, it's very important to note that before you try to simply replace negative thinking with positive thinking, you should first learn to be free from the negative thoughts.

Trying to just replace whatever comparative or otherwise unhelpful thoughts you have with positive thoughts is a lot like putting a bandage on a deep wound that's already infected. The surface of your skin may heal a little faster with a bandage, but underneath the skin is a raging infection that could cause serious problems in the future, like having a limb amputated or even dying.

If you don't take time to allow negative thoughts to unwind and

The Magic of Mindful Self-Awareness

resolve and just try to replace them right away with positive thoughts, those negative thoughts will continue to fester. Eventually, they will come back up into the conscious mind with more power and they'll be even more difficult to deal with. You've probably seen or experienced examples of what happens when people don't properly address negative thoughts or emotions, let them fester, and then snap at some point.

Although there can certainly be value in replacing unhelpful thoughts with more helpful ones (this is actually a core idea in cognitive behavioral therapy), I highly recommend that you don't try to do that right away. First, you need to be free from unhelpful thoughts. You need to remove their power.

Although this is not necessarily easy to do at first, it is actually very simple to do. To be free from thoughts at any moment, all you need to do is become aware of them and see them as objects that arise and pass away in awareness.

There's a catch here, though. If you try to observe your thoughts without first building up a bit of stability of awareness, you'll almost certainly get caught up in those thoughts. They will probably suck you in like a strong riptide in the ocean and entrap you in a negative thought loop.

This is where the practice of mindful self-awareness first reveals its magic.

As the name implies, the practice of mindful self-awareness is the practice of being objectively aware of what we normally think of as being the "self." In my experience, almost every person thinks of himself or herself as the combination of the body, mind, and the contents of the mind, which I'll refer to as "thoughts" for now, for simplicity. Almost everyone spends almost every moment of life *identified with* the body, mind, and thoughts, instead of *being aware of* the body, mind, and thoughts.

Of course, everyone becomes aware of his or her body, mind, and thoughts from time to time, but it tends to happen by accident. There is rarely any intentionality about being mindfully self-aware.

You've probably experienced a moment when you were about to say something. You became aware of your thoughts, realized that what you were about to say was not a skillful thing to say, and decided not to express your thoughts out loud. *That* is mindful self-awareness in action.

Although such random moments of mindful self-awareness can prevent embarrassment and even sometimes save relationships, they have little or no benefit in terms of developing lasting freedom from thoughts.

This is like the difference between running to catch a bus once a week or so and running for three miles, four days a week, every week of the year, for five years. Randomly running to catch a bus doesn't do anything to improve health. However, consistently running for five years would result in significant health benefits, like increased energy, better mood, improved clarity of thought, stronger lungs, a stronger heart, and improved life expectancy.

The practice of mindful self-awareness is the practice of *intentionally* being aware of the body, mind, and thoughts, and developing the ability to be mindfully self-aware for prolonged periods of time with increasingly less effort. In addition to allowing you to be free from thoughts, intentionally developing mindful self-awareness has so many other benefits, supported by a very large body of scientific research, that it almost sounds too good to be true.[2] You'll discover many of those benefits soon.

To be free from thoughts, instead of trying to observe them directly at first, I recommend you start with a more general awareness of the body, for three reasons.

First, thoughts move very fast. When you first start to practice, it can be very hard to keep up with thoughts if you look directly at them. However, the body is very slow-moving, which makes it more useful for building up some stability of awareness.

Second, people tend to be much more identified with thoughts than they are with the body, so thoughts are much more likely to suck you in and trap you in a prolonged internal conversation. While we tend to feel as though that voice in the head is definitely "me," we think of the body in terms of something we own, like "my arm," "my leg," or "my head." Thus, it's much easier to see parts of the body, or even the entire body, objectively.

Third, fortunately, the moment you become aware of your body,

The Magic of Mindful Self-Awareness

you are already peripherally aware of your thoughts. However, with the body as a foundation for mindful self-awareness, you'll be much less likely to get pulled into your thinking and much more likely to develop some stability of awareness.

The following is an exercise that will help you experience the magic of mindful self-awareness, which you can apply to be free from thoughts and stop overthinking at any time. I recommend reading the exercise in its entirety and then giving it a try.

You might even want to record yourself reading the exercise so you can just listen to that guidance while you practice. You can also get free access to a recording of me guiding you through the exercise in the mindful self-awareness section of my website, MattTenney.com.

Although mindful self-awareness can be practiced at any time, we'll start with just sitting still. You don't need to go anywhere special for this. You could just sit in a chair or on your bed. The only thing I recommend you do differently from how you might normally sit is to sit with good posture.

You don't need to be rigid. Just try not to slouch. Sitting with good posture will help you to more easily stabilize awareness. You can practice with your eyes open or closed. However, if your mind is not overwhelmed with thinking, I recommend practicing with eyes closed while sitting still in most cases.

When you're ready to begin, set a timer on your phone for five minutes, and begin.

To start, simply use your inner voice to note what you're doing, "Just sitting." Then, just be open to whatever you notice. You don't need to look for anything to notice, just wait and see what arises.

Try to be like a child who has never sat in the place you're sitting now, so you're truly curious.

For now, if you begin thinking about things, just mentally note, "There is thinking happening. That's OK. Now, I'm just sitting."

During this time of sitting still practice, there's nowhere you need to go. There's nothing you need to do.

This is time for just simply sitting and being.

If you persist with just simply sitting with curiosity for a moment or so, you'll almost certainly notice that the body is breathing while it sits.

Each time it breathes in, it expands a little bit, most noticeably in the belly. Each time it breathes out, it contracts a little bit.

This is not an encouragement to focus on the breath. The breath is just something that can be noticed.

The body is sitting, expanding and contracting.

The expanding and contracting of the body can be used as a nice timer for your effort to practice mindful self-awareness.

You don't need to practice for some long period of time.

You're simply sitting with curiosity for the duration of just one inhalation.

Then, again, for just one exhalation.

Again, you're not focusing on the breath. You're just sitting, using the expanding and contracting body as a timer.

Continue in this way for ten complete breaths.

Now there is some stability of awareness.

You may notice that along with this objective awareness of the body breathing comes an objective awareness of the mind.

You may notice that you see thoughts arising and passing away as though you're watching images on a screen.

You may notice that you can hear the inner voice as though you're listening to sounds coming through speakers or earbuds.

It doesn't matter if there are many thoughts, few thoughts, or no thoughts. All that matters is that you continue observing the body sitting, expanding and contracting.

This provides a foundation for you to see thoughts objectively, without identifying with them.

If you do become entangled with thoughts to the point where you're no longer aware of the expanding and contracting of the body, it's not a problem at all.

This is natural and very likely to occur.

It's also an important part of the practice.

As soon as you notice that you're distracted by thinking, just mentally note, "Oh, I was distracted by thinking. This is not a problem. Now, I'm just sitting," and continue just sitting with curiosity with the next inhalation or exhalation.

Continue in this way until the timer sounds.

The Magic of Mindful Self-Awareness

What did you notice during this exercise? Please take a moment to write down some thoughts about your experience.

If you're like most people who have done this exercise for the first time, you probably noticed that you experienced at least a few brief moments free from your thoughts. You could see them as objects without identifying with them, likely resulting in a significant increase in peace of mind after just a few minutes. (If not, it may be due to ideas you have previously learned about how to practice mindfulness or other forms of meditation. I recommend trying to let go of those ideas and follow the guidance in the exercise above as precisely as possible.)

Hopefully, you have now experienced a small taste of what's possible. You now know that in any moment that isn't very painful physically or emotionally, you can be free from thinking on demand, at least for a brief moment or two.

As you continue to practice in the ways described in the following chapters, it will become easier to be free from your thinking and you'll be able to be free from your thinking in increasingly demanding situations.

Of course, this doesn't happen immediately. The habits of identifying with thinking—which results in overthinking—have likely been continuously reinforced for most of your life. It will take time to break those habits and replace them with the habit of mindful self-awareness.

In the chapters that follow, you'll learn a simple, enjoyable, step-by-step path for doing exactly that. This path won't require you to add anything to your schedule, so you can seamlessly integrate it into your life.

Key Ideas from Chapter 4

1. Ultimately, there is no such thing as a "good" or "bad" experience. What happens to us only appears to be "good" or "bad" based on what happens next.
2. If you can observe thoughts as objects, you can be free from the unhelpful stories people often tell themselves.
3. At first, it's better not to try to directly observe thoughts. Instead, cultivating a general awareness of the body will be easier.

Action Steps for Chapter 4

1. Practice the exercise in this chapter, if you haven't already. A free recording of a guided practice for this is available for download at MattTenney.com.
2. Write down some thoughts about your experience of the practice.

Chapter 5
How to Clear Your Mind and Make the Practice of Mindful Self-Awareness (Almost) Effortless

After completing the exercise described in the last chapter, it's very unlikely that you experienced more than a few brief periods of no thoughts. That's completely normal.

The initial taste of freedom is to simply see thoughts objectively with mindful self-awareness. In any moment that you see thoughts objectively, they have no power over you.

The brief exercise you learned in the last chapter has been refined many times over the last ten years, based on helping thousands of people with the practice. If you'd like to benefit from the practice quickly and avoid potential pitfalls, it's important to practice just the way it's described. There are three main reasons why the practice is described the way it is.

First is the importance of having an attitude of curiosity. The moment you become curious, you let go of identifying with thinking and become mindfully self-aware. A very skillful means for being curious is to maintain a questioning attitude of *What's happening now?* during practice sessions.

Second, mental noting is very powerful for breaking free from identification with thinking. The instant after you use the inner voice to note what the body is doing and/or what's happening in the moment and shift to listening, you drop identification with thought and have an objective self-awareness. It might not last long at first, but that's OK. Little by little, you'll be able to rest in mindful self-awareness for longer and longer periods of time.

Third, you'll notice that I do not recommend trying to focus your attention on an object. Although focusing attention on an object can be a skillful means in the short term in some circumstances—like if you're completely overwhelmed with thinking or a powerful emotion—this type of effort should only be used for short periods of time to build some stability of awareness. Any longer than is needed will do more harm than good.

Many people are taught that they can build up concentration by focusing attention on an object. However, the most sustainable concentration is actually developed effortlessly.

Ultimately, concentration is not something you "do," concentration is something that "happens" when you drop the bad habit of identifying with thinking. After practicing correctly in this way for a sufficient amount of time, awareness can become so stable that it is almost impossible to become distracted.

As a general rule, the only true effort that's needed is to break the habit of identifying with thinking and become mindfully self-aware. This is how you'll most quickly be free from overthinking.

Why the Practice Should Be (Mostly) Effortless

While I was training at the "real" monastery, a very important insight came to me. I was making a strong effort to "pay attention" and "notice things" almost all the time, particularly when we were outside in nature. I noticed that this seemed very tiring. I also felt a lot of disappointment when I did not experience joy after consistently being what I thought was "fully present."

It occurred to me one day that if I wasn't distracted by thinking, I wouldn't have to "try to notice" things. Things in the environment are automatically noticed if we're not distracted by thinking. I realized that all I had to do was become mindfully self-aware, as I did when I first started practicing, which allowed thoughts to be seen as objects.

The Magic of Mindful Self-Awareness

Early on in the practice, especially when there is a lot of thinking going on, it can be helpful to "try to notice" sensations and work to sustain attention on certain ones. This can help calm the mind and build some stability of awareness. However, once some stability of awareness is realized, I recommend letting go of the effort to direct and sustain attention.

I found that the simple shift from making lots of effort to pay attention to just an occasional effort to wake up from distraction resulted in immediately realizing more peace and joy, and in realizing peace and joy for longer periods of time. I later learned of a story that has always helped me remember what the appropriate amount of effort should be during daily life once some stability of awareness is realized.

* * *

There was once an enlightened teacher who many people regard as one of the wisest people to ever live. One day, a king encountered this teacher and a group of his monks. The king noticed that the teacher and his monks radiated peace and joy.

The king asked, "How do you and your monks train to have become such radiant beings?"

The teacher replied, "We practice walking, eating, sitting, cleaning, and other simple activities."

The king said, "But everyone walks. Everyone eats. Everyone sits. Everyone cleans."

The teacher replied, "That is true. However, when we walk, we know that we're walking. When we eat, we know that we're eating. When we sit, we know that we're sitting. When we clean, we know that we're cleaning."

* * *

The story above offers one of the most important points to remember for cultivating freedom from thoughts and unconditional happiness. The practice is not about developing some amazing new skill that requires lots of effort. The practice is about dropping the bad habit of identifying with thinking.

The moment you know what the body is doing—walking, eating, sitting, cleaning, thinking, or whatever else—you drop the bad habit of being identified with thinking, and you become mindfully self-aware. At this point, there's truly nothing more to do. You have achieved the goal.

Although you may not notice at first, once you become mindfully self-aware, self-awareness sustains itself with no further effort from you, for at least a few brief seconds. Then, out of habit, you once again identify with thinking and have to "wake up" again.

This is where the effort comes in. You need to be patient and remember once again to drop identification with thought by applying mental noting and curiosity, gently directing awareness toward your own body. Then, you can just simply let things be as they are.

This is why during the sitting still practice it's so helpful to use the breath as a timer of sorts instead of as an object of attention. By just having a general awareness of what the body is doing, even if it's just sitting still, expanding and contracting, you strike a wonderful balance that allows you to remain mindfully self-aware without building a new bad habit, like trying to maintain focused attention for long periods of time.

A New "Default Mode"

Harvard researcher Matthew Killingsworth has found through his experiments that, on average in a typical day, people are distracted by their thinking 46.9 percent of the time. He also found that this mind wandering is a significant source of unhappiness.[3]

Based on my experience, the "default mode" for almost everyone—whenever they're not engaged in an activity that requires their full attention—is to identify with thinking and get pulled into a conversation in their own mind. The practice of mindful self-awareness is about developing a new default mode of being mindfully self-aware, observing thoughts objectively, instead of being identified with them.

Ultimately, the practice really comes down to this: remembering to wake up and drop your identification with thinking as often as you can. Then, once you're mindfully self-aware, to let go of any mental effort and just let things be as they are.

This is very simple, but it's not easy to do at first. The habit of identifying with thinking is probably the most powerful habit you have. However, as you read the rest of this book and continue practicing what you learn, it will become clear why the practice is really that simple. You'll learn how to make the execution of this simple yet challenging practice so easy that it will gradually become effortless.

How Clearing Your Mind Also Helps You Realize Greater Creativity and Productivity

Many people dream of being able to clear their minds so they can be at peace. Many other people worry that if they have fewer thoughts, or no thoughts, they would lose one of the most valuable tools they have.

Accordingly, I'd like to share some ideas on why developing the ability to clear the mind can actually increase creativity, problem-solving ability, and productivity—in addition to creating peace of mind—and then share important insights for clearing your mind.

Let's start with creativity and problem-solving. Have you ever been struggling to remember someone's name or something else? You keep trying to think of it and, no matter how hard you try, the answer doesn't come to you.

When does the answer come? It often comes the moment you stop trying to think of it, doesn't it?

It seems to me that conscious thinking is actually a hindrance to creativity and that its only value is to help encode thoughts that arise from the subconscious mind into memories that we can readily access again in the future. No great idea or scientific breakthrough I've ever heard of happened while a person was actively thinking about a problem. They all happened when the person was doing something else and was *not actively thinking* about the problem.

By developing the ability to clear your mind of conscious thinking, you actually optimize it for peak performance by allowing a more direct and continuous connection to the subconscious mind, which is infinitely more powerful than conscious thinking. With practice, you'll find that many more creative thoughts arise and that you are able to solve problems more quickly.

This can have a direct impact on productivity, as well. Most people, especially in the West, believe that productivity is the result of doing a lot of stuff. Many people brag about how "crazy busy" they are. These people are often the least productive I know. They spend way too much time doing things that just don't really matter that much.

Productivity is not a function of activity alone. Productivity is a function of identifying and doing what's most important.

Spending all of your time talking to yourself, consciously thinking, is a lot like spending all day obsessively checking email and social media. You're doing a lot of stuff, but it's not stuff that matters much. When you spend all your time on menial tasks, you don't have time to step back and see what's most important.

Similarly, when you spend all your time talking to yourself, consciously thinking, it's as though the mind is so cloudy that you can't make out individual clouds. By learning to clear the mind of conscious thinking, you can start to see individual clouds and identify which ones are most important. By identifying and prioritizing the most important problems and tasks, you can dramatically improve your productivity.

Learning to clear the mind of conscious thinking doesn't mean that thoughts don't arise. Thoughts will still arise from the subconscious mind, and those thoughts tend to be much more useful. Also, the practice of mindful self-awareness will give you the ability to easily let go of thoughts that arise from the subconscious mind in the event they are not useful.

How to Clear Your Mind

Assuming that you're now in agreement that there is no downside to being able to clear your mind of thinking, let's explore how you can clear your mind.

The practice of clearing the mind is very counterintuitive. The most important point to remember is that if you actively try to clear your mind, you will fail. As you'll learn more about in chapter 8, the very act

The Magic of Mindful Self-Awareness

of trying to clear your mind will create the conditions for further identification with thoughts and for endless overthinking.

For now, a simple analogy may be helpful. Imagine a snow globe, a simple toy or ornament that consists of a glass ball filled with liquid and artificial snowflakes, as well as a house or some other object at the bottom. When you shake the snow globe, the water becomes filled with "snowflakes," and there is an appearance of a snowstorm as the "snowflakes" gradually fall down through the water.

Imagine that you wanted to make it so the water was completely clear of "snow," so you tried to force all the "snowflakes" to the bottom by shaking the snow globe with a downward motion. What would happen?

This would result in just perpetually mixing the "snowflakes" in the water. The water would never become clear.

What would happen if you just held the snow globe in your hand and observed it with a patient smile, allowing things to be just as they are?

It wouldn't be long before all the "snowflakes" settled at the bottom of the snow globe and the water was perfectly clear.

This is exactly how the mind works. You cannot make thoughts go away, but you can create the conditions for them to go away on their own by letting go of all mental effort and cultivating the ability to let things be as they are.

Counterintuitively, if you truly want to let something go, the best way to do that is to just *let it be*. You observe it with a patient smile and allow it to be there just the way it is.

You'll learn how to develop this ability more fully as you continue reading and practicing what you learn in this book, starting with the life-changing habit you'll discover in the next chapter.

Key Ideas from Chapter 5

1. The practice of mindful self-awareness can, and should, be almost effortless. Ultimately, the practice is not about acquiring some new skill. It's about dropping the bad habit of identifying with thought.
2. Ultimately, concentration is not something you "do," concentration is something that "happens" when you drop the bad habit of identifying with thinking.
3. Learning to clear your mind and minimize conscious thinking actually improves creativity, clarity of thought, and productivity.
4. If you try to clear your mind, you will fail. This is like trying to make the water in a snow globe clear by trying to force the "snowflakes" to the bottom. Instead, you must learn to objectively observe thoughts just as you would observe a snow globe.
5. The best way to let something go is to let it be exactly as it is.

Action Step for Chapter 5

With the deeper understanding you now have about how to correctly apply mindful self-awareness to be free from thinking and clear your mind, please practice with the five-minute exercise you learned in chapter 4. Please notice whether or not it's easier to become and remain mindfully self-aware.

Chapter 6
The Life-Changing Habit of Taking the Ultimate Vacation Every Day Before Bedtime

Have you ever noticed that many people's vacations go something like the following?

They stress out over how much money they spend on flights and accommodations. They stress out over getting packed. And they stress out trying to navigate the crowds and unfamiliar obstacles they encounter at the airport.

When they finally arrive at their destination, they try to fill every moment with "fun" activities, which often include drinking alcohol (probably in part to let go of the stress that accumulated up to when they arrived). Nothing is quite as "fun" as they hoped it would be (except maybe the drinks).

Then, they go through the travel stress again on their journey home. Once they get home, they stress out even more about how much work they'll have to do to catch up after taking time off.

I've heard more than a few people say that they "need a vacation from their vacation" once they return home.

I apologize if this is how your vacations tend to go. My intent is not to pour salt on an open wound, and I don't mean to discourage anyone from traveling for vacations. In fact, I'm very confident that the practice of mindful self-awareness—and particularly the habits you'll learn in this chapter and the next—will help you transform any travel vacations you take into much more pleasant experiences.

However, there is an even better way to take a vacation. This type of vacation costs nothing, requires no travel, can help improve nearly every aspect of your life, and results in increasingly profound experiences of well-being. This is why I call it *the ultimate vacation*.

If you think about what you'd want from the perfect vacation—assuming your intent is to relax and recharge—I believe you'd agree that what you're really looking for is a chance to *just simply be*. Our lives are filled with almost constant doing, much of it reacting to what other people are asking of us. So, the perfect vacation would be one that gives us the opportunity to be free from the constant doing and reacting, and simply enjoy *being* in a beautiful, relaxing place.

If this resonates with you, I have some very good news! It's possible to experience such a true vacation every day, no matter where you are, with the practice of mindful self-awareness.

A Life-Changing Meta Habit

In this book, I repeatedly stress the importance of developing habits. Reading this book will do nothing for you, other than inspire you for a while, unless you take the steps necessary to form new, helpful habits and let go of old, unhelpful habits.

Following is the first habit I'm going to share, which is perhaps the most important habit you'll learn in this book in terms of your overall health and success in life. It is the habit of practicing mindful self-awareness while sitting still for at least five minutes every night before you lie down to go to sleep.

Before I share the details of building this habit, I'd like to share why it's so incredibly powerful.

First, this is truly the ultimate vacation. There's nothing you have to do, nowhere you have to go, and it requires no money. All you have to do is *just be*.

Second, this practice allows you to discover that *just being* is very relaxing. In fact, it's all you need to experience complete satisfaction. All

The Magic of Mindful Self-Awareness

the amazing experiences you can have in life become icing on the cake when you learn how to be completely satisfied with *just being*.

Third, this practice will help you to strengthen your ability to be mindfully self-aware. This allows you to be free from thinking on demand, and more frequently.

Fourth, although it may sound like you're giving up five minutes of sleep, you'll actually end up getting more sleep and better sleep.

If you're like many people, it may take many minutes to fall asleep because you're thinking about all sorts of things while lying in bed. By trading the first five minutes of lying down for sitting still practice, you may actually end up gaining ten or twenty minutes of sleep.

Getting good sleep is absolutely essential for being as healthy and successful as possible, particularly for reducing anxiety. Anxiety often creates a vicious cycle that spins into depression.

If you're anxious during the day it becomes harder to sleep at night, particularly if the anxiety lasts long enough to result in cortisol being at levels that are higher than needed. (Most people probably fall into this category, stating stress has the biggest impact on their mental health, according to the American Psychiatric Association's annual mental health poll.[4]) The less sleep you get, the more anxious you feel. The more anxious you feel, the harder it is to sleep at night.

However, the reverse is also true. By becoming free from anxious thoughts with the practice of mindful self-awareness, it's much easier to fall asleep fast, which results in more sleep. The practice can also help you to get better sleep because you're less likely to wake up in the middle of the night with anxious thoughts. Getting more and better sleep then makes it easier to be free from anxiety the next day, which makes it easier to fall asleep at night, and so on.

This is why the practice of sitting still in mindful self-awareness before bed is what habits expert Charles Duhigg calls a meta habit, or keystone habit. This one habit of sitting still in mindful self-awareness right before bed makes it easier to start and maintain many other good habits.

The fifth reason this is such a great habit is that bedtime is probably the time you can most easily control. You almost certainly go to sleep every night. All you need to do is trade the first five minutes of lying down for five minutes of practicing mindful self-awareness while sitting still on your bed. This is the best way I know of to build the daily habit of sitting still practice, which is an essential part of realizing all the benefits you learn about in this book.

Why Practicing Mindful Self-Awareness Right Before Bedtime Satisfies All Four of the Laws for Habit Formation

By practicing right before bed, you'll satisfy all four of the laws for habit formation that James Clear describes in his excellent best-selling book, *Atomic Habits*.

Practicing right before bed makes the practice obvious. It's hard to forget because you have to sit in bed before you lie down (unless you're one of those fun people who just jump into a lying position in bed each night).

Practicing right before bed makes the practice attractive. You know you'll be able to fall asleep faster if you let your mind unwind for a few minutes before lying down.

Practicing right before bed makes the practice easy. You don't have to add anything to your schedule. You're just trading five minutes of lying down for five minutes of sitting still in mindful self-awareness.

Finally, practicing right before bed makes the practice satisfying for at least two reasons: you'll feel a deeper sense of peace and well-being after each practice session, and you'll get more and better sleep, which will help you feel better and perform better the next day.

How to Practice Taking the Ultimate Vacation

Following are some recommendations for building this life-changing habit.

First, please create an alarm on your phone right now for one hour before you plan to go to bed. If you're close to bedtime now, please set one for the next day. Name the alarm "Ultimate Vacation."

For extra credit, if you're interested in realizing the incredible power of getting better sleep—like dramatically reducing anxiety and

The Magic of Mindful Self-Awareness

improving productivity—try to stop looking at screens after your Ultimate Vacation alarm goes off. Two of the most important things you can do for getting better sleep are to go to bed at the same time every night, ideally early enough to allow you to get at least seven hours of sleep, and to stop looking at screens at least one hour before bedtime.

Second, try to use something other than your phone as a timer for the sitting still practice so you don't have to interact with your phone right before bed. You could use a watch or an analog timer of some type.

If you absolutely must use your phone as the timer, please put your phone in airplane mode when your Ultimate Vacation alarm goes off one hour before bed, and set your timer to five minutes then. That way, you'll be much less likely to interact with your phone right before bed, and you'll only need to glance at your phone briefly to start the timer. You should be able to stop the timer without even looking at your phone.

Third, start with committing to just five minutes of practice. This is something that is very easy to commit to and stick with. You'll be much more likely to form this life-changing habit if you start with just five minutes, instead of committing to ten or fifteen or more.

You may end up practicing more than five minutes on some or many nights, but the most important step for now is to form a consistent habit of practicing for at least five minutes every night, whether you feel like doing it or not. Once having an Ultimate Vacation before bed becomes a habit, because it's so pleasant and has so many benefits, you'll probably want to practice for longer periods of time by either starting a little earlier or practicing until you're feeling sleepy.

Fourth, start your timer, and use the practice you learned in chapter 4 or another practice you learn later in the book. Again, you can get free access to recorded guided practices at MattTenney.com.

Fifth, although this habit is quite self-reinforcing because it feels good and helps you get better sleep, in order to have the best chance of making this a lasting habit, I strongly recommend that you let a couple of friends or family members know that you're doing this practice and ask if any of them would like to form the same habit. You could check in on each other every few days to discuss how it's going and how many nights in a row you've practiced.

Please text a few friends or family members right now to start this conversation.

Sixth, if you haven't already, download the free *The Magic of Mindful Self-Awareness Practice Tracker* calendar from MattTenney.com. This will allow you to track how many nights in a row you've kept the habit of taking the Ultimate Vacation before you lie down for bed.

Seeing your progress on this tracker is another way to make your new habit satisfying and ensure the practice becomes a habit. There is something quite satisfying about having a visual reminder of progress.

Although seeing your progress on the practice tracker is satisfying in and of itself, you might also want to take a picture of your progress every day and share it on social media. This will help you stick with the practice and give your friends a chance to help encourage you to keep the practice going. As a side benefit, you may end up helping a few friends start the practice, too!

The Magic of Mindful Self-Awareness

Key Ideas for Chapter 6

1. Practicing the "Ultimate Vacation" before bed is a meta habit: one good habit that makes it easier to start and maintain many other good habits.
2. By following the action steps for this chapter, you'll be much more likely to build and maintain a life-changing habit.

Action Steps for Chapter 6

1. Create an alarm on your phone for one hour before bed to remind you to practice the Ultimate Vacation.
2. Follow the guidance in this chapter for practicing the Ultimate Vacation and tracking and sharing your progress. You can find the free practice tracker and free recorded guided practices to use during your Ultimate Vacation practice time at MattTenney.com.

Chapter 7

An Extraordinary Paradigm Shift: How to Transform Mundane Activities Into Magical Moments and Be Happy 95% of the Time

Prior to living and training as a monk, as far back as I can remember, I looked to the future for happiness. I thought happiness was dependent on certain conditions being met.

When I was in grade school, I remember thinking how big and cool the middle school kids seemed to be. They almost seemed like adults. I thought that once I was in middle school, my life would probably be so much better.

When I got to middle school, I realized that things were pretty much the same. We didn't really seem like adults. I wasn't satisfied.

While in middle school, I noticed how much bigger and cooler the high school kids seemed to be. They really seemed like adults. They could even drive cars! I thought for sure that once I was in high school, my life would be much better.

Once I got to high school, although some of it was great, much of it was painful and stressful. I still wasn't satisfied.

I thought for sure, though, that once I went off to college I would finally be truly happy.

After I started college at the University of Minnesota, it wasn't long before I thought I would be happier someplace else. When I transferred universities, it wasn't long before I started thinking how much happier I

The Magic of Mindful Self-Awareness

would be after I graduated and was commissioned as an officer in the Marine Corps. And, of course, it wasn't long after joining the Marine Corps that I started thinking about how much happier I would be once I got out.

When I first started reflecting on this, I realized that this habit of looking to the future for happiness wasn't just something I did in terms of periods of life. I was almost always looking to the future for happiness, particularly during the simple, mundane moments of life, like cleaning the floors, washing the dishes, or brushing my teeth.

I would always rush through the mundane moments to get on to what appeared to be the "exciting" future. For instance, I would think that once I finished washing the dishes and started watching a football game, then I would be happy. While I was washing the dishes, I would be so lost in thought that it was almost as though I wasn't really there.

I now realize what a terrible habit this is.

I would estimate that, for the average person, only about 5 percent of life consists of very pleasurable or very painful experiences. I estimate that, for the average person, about 95 percent of life consists of simple mundane moments like brushing your teeth, cleaning, walking from place to place, working, sitting and waiting, or driving a car. So, if you're not present during these moments, not living them, it means that in your rush to get to the "exciting future," you're skipping over about 95 percent of your life!

The biggest problem with looking to the future for happiness is that the future isn't promised to any of us. We tend to live as though we're going to be alive as humans on earth forever, but our time here will definitely come to an end. It could be decades from now, or it could be tomorrow. I think it's a very risky bet to consistently look to the future for happiness when there's no guarantee that the future will ever arrive.

Also, upon reflection, it's clear that the future never *truly* arrives because, when we actually experience what used to be in the future, it has become the present. We only ever truly experience what's happening in the present moment.

Unfortunately, the brain is a very habitual machine. As long as the habitual way of living is to look to the future for happiness or have other conditions for happiness, then you'll never be happy.

Once the future you've been looking forward to arrives, you'll realize you're not satisfied and start looking for some other condition you'll need to meet to be happy, like a future milestone. Once you get that thing you want, you'll start looking for the next thing. For many people, this cycle never ends, even when they achieve their "dreams."

For instance, I had a friend in the Marine Corps who had trained most of his life to become the national champion for running the ten-kilometer event in track and field. While in college, he realized his goal and became the national champion for men under twenty-one.

He told me that within a couple of days of winning the championship, he fell into a deep depression. He started looking for what he could do next and had no idea what his "next" would be. His depression lasted for months.

Similarly, you've probably heard many stories of people winning millions of dollars in the lottery and experiencing a short burst of happiness. Then, within a year, they return to the same level of general happiness they had before winning the lottery. In fact, some even become depressed when they realize that even millions of dollars didn't bring them lasting happiness.

An Extraordinary Paradigm Shift

If you're like nearly everyone I've ever talked to about this, you are probably not as present as you'd like to be during the mundane moments of life because you're thinking about other things and often rushing through those moments to get to the "exciting future."

Let's consider brushing your teeth, for example. What is this experience generally like for you?

If you're like nearly everyone I've talked to about this, you probably think about all sorts of things while brushing your teeth. You may even become so distracted by thinking sometimes that you forget which teeth you've brushed and need to start over. And, you likely rush to get your teeth brushed so you can move on to what's really important or "exciting" in the future.

Although you might not have noticed this in the moment, when you're caught up in thinking and/or rushing to the future, you actually

The Magic of Mindful Self-Awareness

create a little bit of anxiety. Unfortunately, anxiety is cumulative. The more mundane moments you rush through or experience only partially because you're caught up in thinking, the more anxious you will become throughout the day. Many people finish the day needing to unwind their anxiety, which they often try to do with entertainment or intoxicants.

This habit of skipping over the mundane moments of life because we're caught up in thinking while rushing through them to get to the future is extremely detrimental to being happy. This habit causes us to constantly add to our anxiety. It also causes us to rush toward a future that may never come and which, even if it does come, won't bring us lasting happiness.

What if all of this could be completely reversed?

Thanks to the powerful practice of mindful self-awareness, it is possible to transform the mundane moments of life from moments that increase anxiety and strengthen bad habits into magical moments that will help you to realize many, many benefits, including the following.

First, by practicing mindful self-awareness during the mundane moments of life, those moments are no longer just obstacles in the way of a more important or exciting future. Those moments become opportunities to systematically develop the most important skills there are for both personal and professional success, like self-awareness, kindness, generosity, and compassion.

Self-awareness is arguably the most important skill you can develop for both personal and professional success. It is the key to knowing your strengths and weaknesses, for putting together great teams, and for making good decisions. It is also the foundation of emotional intelligence, which is extremely important for being successful in life. Every emotional intelligence competency relies on the foundation of self-awareness.

Also, regardless of what, if any, spiritual tradition you come from, I'm very confident you would agree that the qualities of kindness, generosity, and compassion are the most important qualities you can develop as a human being. The practice of mindful self-awareness is a systematic way of training to develop those qualities.

As a Christian, I believe that our highest calling is to be as Christlike as possible and work to cultivate the qualities of kindness, generosity, compassion, and even unconditional love for all people. My spiritual life became very energized when I realized that the practice of mindful self-awareness is a systematic way of training to become more Christlike.

Second, when you're caught up in thinking, the mundane moments of life tend to be just another part of the day that increases your anxiety levels, negatively impacting your well-being and making you less effective at whatever you do next. But when you practice mindful self-awareness during those moments, they become opportunities to actually lower your anxiety levels. They therefore have a positive impact on your well-being and help you to be more effective at whatever you're going to do next.

Third, by practicing mindful self-awareness during the mundane moments of life, you start to discover peace of mind, and even joy, in moments that you used to see as obstacles to what you wanted. This allows you to directly realize that you can be happy regardless of what situation you find yourself in.

You'll realize, just as I did when I was in prison, that if you're just brushing your teeth, not caught in your thoughts of past or future, joy is possible while brushing your teeth at any time, no matter what is happening in your life outside of that moment. Since roughly 95 percent of your life consists of simple, mundane moments, like brushing your teeth, this means that you can be happy during at least 95 percent of your life!

Perhaps most important, by practicing mindful self-awareness during the mundane moments of life, you'll no longer be skipping over most of your life, rushing toward a future that may never come. Instead, you'll be truly living in each moment. You'll be fully present during those moments, which will help you develop the habit of being present all the time, including during time spent interacting with other people.

When you spend time with people you love, you'll actually be there, fully present, instead of being partially or completely caught up in thoughts. As a result, people will feel more loved by you, and your relationships will deepen and become significantly more fulfilling.

Thanks to the magic of mindful self-awareness, you can transform the mundane moments of life from moments that are principal causes of suffering in life into moments that are principal causes of happiness, success, and fulfillment. The practice of mindful self-awareness during mundane daily activities can help you create this extraordinary paradigm shift.

How to Realize the Magic of Mindful Self-Awareness During Mundane Daily Activities

The first step I recommend for building your practice of mindful self-awareness during daily activities is to make a list, in chronological order, of all the activities you do on a daily basis in relative solitude (at first, it's easier to practice when you don't feel required to interact with other people).

The list would likely include things like getting dressed, brushing your teeth, taking a shower, washing your hands, drinking water or some other liquid, eating breakfast, cleaning dishes, sitting in your car or some form of public transportation, walking to your office, or walking from some other place to another place.

Once you have your list, please pick just one activity to start with for the first week and write it down on *The Magic of Mindful Self-Awareness Practice Tracker*. Ideally, you would pick the first activity on the list, but let's use brushing your teeth as an example.

After you've added "brushing your teeth" in the appropriate spot on the practice tracker, please also create a sticky note, or a note you could hang up with tape, to remind you to practice mindful self-awareness while you brush your teeth. I recommend adding a little smiley face to the note to remind you that it's possible to be happy right now.

Then put the note right on your toothpaste or on the mirror you see when brushing your teeth. The next time you brush your teeth, you'll be reminded to practice mindful self-awareness during that activity.

Following is some guidance on how to practice mindful self-awareness while brushing your teeth, which you can modify as needed for any activity in the day.

Start by simply mentally noting "brushing the teeth." Then, just observe yourself with mindful self-awareness—with an attitude of curiosity—putting on the toothpaste, brushing your teeth, rinsing the brush, and turning off the water. Be like a child who has never brushed her or his teeth before.

At first, it may be helpful to "try to notice" sensations and maintain awareness of pleasant or neutral sensations.

With continued practice, however, you won't need to "try to notice" sensations. The moment you wake up to mindful self-awareness, you are no longer distracted. You are fully present and you'll notice—without even trying—many little details of the experience you normally miss.

Thoughts are going to arise. This is perfectly natural and not a problem.

When thoughts arise, just mentally note "Thinking about (insert topic)," allow the thought to be there just as it is, and then note, "Now, just brushing the teeth again."

Thoughts may arise many times while brushing your teeth for the recommended two minutes. This is not a problem.

Be curious about them just as you are about other sensations and, most importantly, the general awareness you have of the entire body during this activity.

At first, it will likely feel as though you are constantly noting thoughts and trying to redirect your awareness to observe yourself. It will seem like observing yourself in activity takes effort.

However, with practice, you'll notice that once you wake up to mindful self-awareness, there's no more effort needed. You "know you are brushing your teeth." You'll notice that there's an objective self-awareness—awareness of the body and thinking—naturally occurring without any additional effort.

You'll surely be distracted again, but you can just rinse and repeat the following: note that you're thinking, note what you're doing, and rest in the refuge of mindful self-awareness that naturally persists on its own for a few seconds or minutes.

Gradually, with consistent practice, the periods of time in between being distracted and redirecting awareness, in which you are effortlessly self-aware, will become longer and longer. The practice will take increasingly less effort.

For the first week, at the end of each day right before practicing mindful self-awareness while sitting still before bed, check the boxes on

The Magic of Mindful Self-Awareness

the practice tracker for the day if you practiced mindful self-awareness while brushing your teeth that day and while sitting still before bed the evening before.

After the first week, please pick a second activity from your list of daily activities, ideally the second activity in chronological order, and add it to the practice tracker along with the activity you chose for week one (in this example, brushing your teeth). Let's use getting dressed as an example. After adding "getting dressed" to the practice tracker, create and place your note in a good spot to remind you to practice with this new activity, like near the light switch for your closet or handle for a drawer.

During week two, you would continue to practice mindful self-awareness while brushing your teeth, as described above, and also practice while getting dressed. At the end of each day, if you practiced while brushing your teeth and getting dressed that day, and sitting still the evening before, you would check the appropriate boxes on the practice tracker.

Each week, please continue practicing during the activities you've already started and add one new activity until you've added every activity from your list. Continue to track your progress on the practice tracker.

The New Default Mode Is Happiness

For most people I observe, when they are not engaged in some activity, they are either lost in thought or using a device of some type. This is why they don't discover sustainable, unconditional happiness. Their default mode is to do things that make them more anxious, as discussed in chapter 5.

It's not the thinking or the devices that are the problems. It's the relationship people have with those things.

When we're identified with our thoughts and emotions, instead of seeing thoughts and emotions objectively with mindful self-awareness, we become prisoners of those thoughts, subject to whatever emotions they trigger in us. Similarly, instead of seeing smartphones as powerful tools for productivity and connection, many people are chained to them like prisoners, reacting to them constantly and going to them for distraction whenever they feel the slightest bit bored.

With mindful self-awareness, you come to see thinking as a tool that you can use when needed and drop when not needed. Likewise, you can use devices with greater intentionality and freedom. You might decide to check devices once every couple of hours, or once every hour, while being mindfully self-aware during the time you spend using them. In this way, both thoughts and devices become tools that add value and happiness, instead of distraction and anxiety.

After about ninety days of practicing in the way described above with the twelve or so activities on your list, you will have formed a very solid foundation for practicing mindful self-awareness. Those twelve activities will serve as anchors for you.

Even if you never remember to be mindfully self-aware during the time you use a device, or any other activity during the day that's not on your list, the time you practice while sitting still and during the twelve or so activities on your practice tracker will make a huge impact on your happiness levels.

Also, without being so formal about it, although you certainly could be if you like, you'll find that you're starting to practice mindful self-awareness during more and more activities that weren't on your list, including while using devices and even during interactions with other people. You may discover that being mindfully self-aware has become your new default mode of being.

Instead of feeling trapped inside your head nearly all the time, you'll notice that you see your thoughts objectively nearly all the time, often without making any effort to do so. You'll thereby be free from your thoughts. When this happens, you will realize unconditional happiness during about 95 percent of your life.

The Magic of Mindful Self-Awareness

Key Ideas from Chapter 7

1. Most people have the habit of placing conditions on their happiness, believing that they'll be happier in the future. Thus, they are never satisfied.
2. Although the habit of looking to the future for happiness is not easy to break, it can be broken. It's possible to be happy now.
3. For most people, the mundane moments of life, which probably constitute about 95 percent of life for the average person, are moments that we rush through to get on to the important or exciting moments we anticipate in the future. This means that the mundane moments of life are adding to our anxiety and strengthening bad habits. It also means that we're skipping over 95 percent of our lives in our rush toward the future.
4. Thanks to the practice of mindful self-awareness during daily, mundane activities, it's possible to transform those activities into opportunities to build life-changing habits, reduce anxiety, and realize happiness during 95 percent of life!

Action Step from Chapter 7

Please follow the guidance in this chapter to make your chronological list of mundane daily activities and add the first one to your daily practice tracker.

A Special Action Step

Before you go on to part 3 of this book, I'd like to offer a way for you to add value to the lives of others.

If you found this book helpful, and think it will be helpful to others, there's an easy way for you to help other people find the book.

Please leave an honest review of this book on Amazon.com that includes at least a couple of sentences sharing your thoughts on the book.

There's a QR code linking to the Amazon.com review section below.

Please scan the code with the camera on your phone, tap the link that appears on your phone, and take 60 seconds to leave your review.

Every review—including yours—makes an impact by helping more people find the book on Amazon.com.

I would personally be very grateful to you for leaving an honest review.

More importantly, other people will be thankful to you because you will have helped them discover a book that could significantly change their lives for the better.

Thank you in advance, my friend!

Please Scan Me to Leave a Review

Part Three

Awakening to Your True Self: How to Be at Peace During the 5% of Life That Is Truly Painful and Live a Deeply Meaningful Life

Chapter 8
The Wisdom That Frees You from All Suffering: Realizing Your True Self

There's a story of a young actress named Mary, who had a life with almost no problems to speak of. She wanted to get a part in a major motion picture. She believed that this would be her big break and help her to become a star.

She was going to play the part of a woman named Amy, who had all sorts of problems in life. Amy had just lost her job, her boyfriend left her, and she ended up homeless.

Mary studied the character several hours each day for months to prepare for her audition. Nevertheless, she wanted an extra edge to ensure she would get the part. She decided to hire a hypnotist to help her.

The hypnotist agreed to hypnotize Mary so that she would truly believe she was Amy, the character she would be playing in the movie. From the moment she was hypnotized, she became a completely different person. She became Amy.

Amy worried constantly. She had so many problems to deal with that she didn't know where to begin. She suffered a great deal.

Unfortunately for Mary, soon after being hypnotized, the hypnotist died in an accident. Mary, who had a wonderful life, was now stuck being Amy, who was experiencing a very difficult time in life.

As bad as the situation seems in the fictional story above, Amy could be free from all her suffering in an instant if the hypnotist could just snap his fingers and allow her to see the truth: Amy is not her true self. Amy is just a part Mary is playing for a short period of time.

Just like Amy, you can be free from your suffering the moment you realize that this life as a human being is just a part you're playing for a short period of time. Your true self—your eternal or spiritual self—is ultimately not affected by what happens to the body and mind. Your true self does not suffer. Your true self is always at peace.

In this chapter, you'll discover how to realize your true self and how to be your true self with increasing frequency. You'll also discover why this is the key to being at peace, and potentially even happy, during even the 5 percent of life that is very painful physically or emotionally.

Pain Is Objective and Mandatory—Suffering Is Subjective and Optional

As I first wrote twenty years ago in my first draft of *A Practical Guide to True Happiness and Freedom*, and I'm sure many people have written before and since, pain is an objective experience that is inevitable. As long as you're alive in a human body with a functioning nervous system you're going to experience pain, both physically and emotionally.

However, it is possible to experience pain without suffering at all.

Let's use the example of touching something hot with your hand as an example. When you touch something hot, a nerve sends a message to an interneuron in your spinal cord. This interneuron sends a message to the muscles that control the hand and arm causing them to pull away from the hot object. Your brain then receives a message regarding the potential damage to the body, which you perceive as pain.

The process described above is objective and mandatory for anyone with a functioning nervous system. However, what happens next is subjective.

You might start yelling and screaming and get very angry, all of which increases the severity and duration of your perceived pain. You could suffer a great deal. Or, you could simply notice that there's a red

The Magic of Mindful Self-Awareness

mark on your hand and go right back to whatever you were going to do next. You don't suffer at all.

Although there's a little more nuance to this, which I share below, at the most basic level, suffering is the mental struggle—or even anguish—that comes with wanting something other than what's happening in the present moment. If you *don't want* what's happening to you in the present moment to happen, you suffer.

For instance, here's a silly but poignant example. Imagine you told a friend that you are running an experiment. You ask her to slap you in the face so you can see how it feels. She obliges and slaps you with a decent amount of force. You certainly feel some pain, but you don't suffer. You might even laugh and say, "Wow. That was a good slap!"

Now imagine that you're walking on a street one day, and a stranger just randomly slaps you in the face for no apparent reason. It hurts just the same, but you get really upset. You might suffer a great deal.

What's the difference between the two scenarios above?

In the first scenario, you were OK with the experience. In the second scenario, you didn't want it to happen.

Here's a more realistic example. Imagine a father of five young children who has been dealing with whining, crying, and screaming kids all day. When this father finally gets a break from taking care of the children, he goes out to the garage to sit in his car and enjoy ten minutes of silence. The experience of sitting in a quiet car that isn't moving would probably seem pretty close to heaven relative to the chaos of the rest of the day.

Imagine then, the next day, that same father is late for work, and he gets stuck in a traffic jam. The cars aren't moving at all. He really wants to get to work, so he gets very anxious and even angry. His anxiety and frustration continue to grow as long as he's focused on wanting to get to work.

What's the difference between the two scenarios above?

In the first scenario, the father was perfectly OK being in a car that wasn't moving. In the second scenario, he didn't want to be in a car that wasn't moving.

I'm not suggesting that you can be free from the suffering that often arises during or after a traumatic experience by somehow tricking yourself into being "OK" with it happening. The two scenarios above are used just to illustrate how pain is objective and suffering is subjective.

To be free from suffering, you just need to let go of the desire to have something other than what's currently happening.

The Immediate Cause of Suffering

The immediate cause of suffering is identifying with a desire and thereby getting caught up in it. To be free from suffering in any moment, then, all you need to do is become mindfully self-aware and thereby see the desire objectively.

To be clear, I'm not saying that you shouldn't have desires. It's perfectly fine to want things to be a certain way and to have goals. What I am saying is that if you identify with and attach to a desire or a goal in a given moment, you will suffer in that moment. (Also, as you'll discover in chapter 10, you'll be more likely to achieve your goals if you're not attached to them.)

To be free from suffering, you need to change your relationship with the desires that arise within you.

The correct relationship with a desire is to see it as a tool that exists to compel you to take some sort of action. If you see a desire objectively, allowing it to arise and pass away, then the desire does not control you. You have the choice to decide whether or not you want to act on that desire. Also, when you have such an objective view of a desire, whether you take action or not, there is no suffering.

However, if you identify with the desire as being "me" or "mine," the desire will negatively impact your state of mind and control your behavior. You will be doomed to suffer until you either gratify the desire or see it objectively.

Following are two examples to help you see how this works, one example of wanting to get rid of something and one example of wanting to obtain something you don't have. Let's start with wanting to obtain something you don't have, like your favorite food. In my case, it would be an Indian dish called chana masala. Maybe yours is ice cream.

Imagine you're engaged in some activity that you enjoy, like walking in the woods, when the thought of having ice cream arises. Because you

The Magic of Mindful Self-Awareness

really like ice cream, the desire to have it immediately arises, which is natural. However, the moment you identify with the desire to have the ice cream, you will start to suffer.

There will be tension in the mind and body that won't go away until you either eat the ice cream or become free from the desire. As long as you're attached to the desire to have ice cream, the walk you were enjoying will be nothing more than an obstacle to you getting what you want.

Also, because you've reinforced the habit of seeking happiness by gratifying your desires, the ice cream will not satisfy you for long. Soon after eating the ice cream, you'll experience a void that yearns to be filled. This will lead to a desire for something else. If you identify with that desire, you'll be caught in suffering once again.

However, if when the desire to have ice cream first arises, you see it as an object that simply arises and passes away, there is no tension in the body and mind. You do not suffer. The desire may compel you to make a note to pick up ice cream on the way home, but it doesn't detract from your walk in the woods.

Additionally, because you strengthened the habit of being present with and enjoying what you're doing now, it's less likely that you'll be bothered if you don't get the ice cream. Moreover, if you do get the ice cream, you'll enjoy it even more because you'll be less likely to be thinking about other things while you eat it.

Now let's explore wanting to get rid of something unpleasant, like an itch.

Imagine you have an itch, which is actually a mild form of pain, in the middle of your back. Because it's unpleasant, you want to get rid of it, which is natural. However, the moment you identify with the desire to get rid of the itch, you will start to suffer. There will be tension in the mind and body that doesn't go away until you get rid of the itch.

Also, because you've reinforced the habit of seeking happiness by gratifying your desires, you'll be more likely to be stuck in suffering again the moment you experience something unpleasant, like another itch.

However, if when the desire to get rid of the itch first arises, or anytime thereafter, you see the desire as an object that simply arises and passes away in awareness, the tension in the body will immediately begin to unwind. The suffering will cease. You'll realize that you can be perfectly at peace with an itch on your back.

Also, because you've reinforced the habit of being free from desires by seeing them objectively with mindful self-awareness, you'll be less likely to suffer the next time something unpleasant happens. You'll be one step closer to freedom from all suffering.

At this point, you may have just had an epiphany that is very exciting. You may now see that while pain is an unavoidable part of life, it is actually quite possible to be completely free from suffering. You just need to train to see desires objectively instead of identifying with them.

Of course, this is much easier said than done. The habit of identifying with desires as being "me" or "mine" has likely been reinforced your entire life since a very young age. It will take some time and effort to break that habit and replace it with the habit of seeing desires objectively with mindful self-awareness.

Fortunately, there is a way to make it much easier to break the habit of identifying with and being controlled by desires. It starts with understanding the root cause of suffering.

The Root Cause of Suffering: Identifying with a False Sense of Self

As you may recall from the story above about Mary the actress who thought she was Amy, all of her suffering would have ended the moment she woke up from hypnosis and realized that she was actually Mary and only playing the part of Amy for a short time. In a general sense, almost everyone on this planet suffers from a similar affliction.

If you're like most people I've discussed this with, you probably believe and even understand intellectually that there is some aspect of you that is more enduring than your human body and its thoughts. This is what most people refer to as the *true self* or *spiritual self*. Although you may believe that such a true self exists, you may not know how to intentionally realize your true self.

You probably spend most of your time living as though your true self is the human body and the thoughts created by your brain. This

The Magic of Mindful Self-Awareness

sense of "me" is often referred to as the ego. Identification with the ego as being the true self is the root cause of suffering.

Returning to the example of experiencing an itch will help demonstrate why identifying with the ego is the root cause of suffering. If you're identified with the ego as being your true self, when an itch first arises, your perception will be *I have an itch*. If your perception is *I have an itch*, then a feeling of aversion will almost certainly arise. It is natural to dislike unpleasant experiences.

If you identify with the feeling of *I don't like this itch*, then a desire to get rid of the itch will almost certainly arise. It's natural to want to get rid of things you don't like.

But the moment you identify with the desire to get rid of the itch, you will start to suffer. There will be tension in the mind and body that won't go away until you get rid of the itch.

However, as you read above in the section about the immediate cause of suffering, if you don't identify with the desire as being "me" or "mine," but see it as an object that simply arises and passes away in awareness, there will be no suffering. A feeling of dislike wouldn't even arise.

Likewise, if a feeling of dislike did arise but you didn't identify with the feeling of *I don't like this itch*, then the desire to get rid of the itch would not arise. Why would you want to get rid of something if there's no feeling of aversion toward it?

It is probably now clear why the way to remove the root cause of suffering is to realize your true self. In any moment that you are being your true self without identifying with the ego, suffering cannot arise.

If you're not identified with the ego, when the sensation of the itch first arises your perception is not *I have an itch*. Instead, since the true self is not ultimately affected by what happens to the physical body, the perception is simply *There is an itch happening*. If there is no thought of a "me" to whom the itch is happening, a feeling of like or dislike will not arise.

If a feeling of dislike doesn't arise, then the desire to get rid of the itch won't arise. If there's no desire to get rid of the itch, then there's no problem, is there? There is no suffering. You can be perfectly at peace while experiencing an itch.

If you can be at peace with an itch, which is a mild form of pain, you can be at peace with more severe forms of pain as well. Many people have trained their minds to be able to experience extreme pain while remaining perfectly calm and at peace. They don't suffer at all during such an experience.

Of course, I'm not recommending that you should endure extreme pain to test this out. Training with itches is sufficient.

However, I hope it is now clear that you can, in fact, be free from all suffering. All you need to do is break the habit of identifying with the ego as being your true self by more regularly seeing clearly that this false sense of "me" is not ultimately you.

Awakening to Your True Self

Breaking the habit of identifying with the ego as being your true self is not easy. You've likely spent nearly your entire life identified with this false sense of "me" as being your true self.

However, the process of breaking the habit of identifying with the ego is simple. You just need to practice being mindfully aware of what you normally think of as being your "self"—the sense of "me" that we call the ego—as often as possible, and for increasingly longer periods of time.

I recommend starting the practice of mindful self-awareness by having a general awareness of the body. However, as you progress you'll need to learn to direct awareness a little more pointedly at the aspect of yourself that feels most like the sense of "me" with which you identify the most.

If you're like most people, you're probably not most identified with the body as being the "me." We tend to see the body as something the ego, the "me," owns. We refer to the hand as "my" hand. We refer to the heart as "my" heart. We refer to the brain as "my" brain.

This language is more than just semantics. It is very telling.

We feel as though there is some "me" that is somehow in the body but at the same time owns the body. It's as though the body is carrying this "me" around like the body is some type of vehicle.

The Magic of Mindful Self-Awareness

However, this sense of "me" is nothing more than the ego, a bundle of thoughts. It is not your true self.

I'm not saying that there isn't a part of you that is spiritual, and perhaps eternal. I am saying with certainty that the sense of "me" you experience, which seems to own your hand, your heart, and your brain, is not the true, spiritual self. It is just the ego.

Fortunately, this is not something you need to just believe. This is something that you can, and should, verify through your own experience. Some simple thought experiments can help make this truth crystal clear, at least at the intellectual level.

Imagine that you're sitting still and there's not a single thought in your mind. There is just a pure awareness of whatever sensations are arising and passing away. Then, a thought about eating ice cream arises. *I really like ice cream*, your inner voice says. Then, the voice goes silent and you're once again sitting with a mind that is empty of thought.

You existed and were experiencing the world when the mind was empty of thought. You existed when the thought was present. And, you still existed after thinking ceased and the mind was empty once again.

What does this tell you about who you are?

This simple thought experiment tells you that you are not the voice in your head, which is what people tend to identify with most as being "me." That voice is something that arises and passes away with no effect on whether or not you still exist and experience the world.

Similarly, when you were three months old, there was no inner voice commenting on everything. You didn't have the capacity for language at that age.

Your current sense of "me" did not exist when you were three months old. It wasn't created by your brain until after you developed the capacity for thought.

Yet, clearly, some aspect of who you are now existed when you were three months old, didn't it? Isn't a three-month-old baby just as much a human as a person who is thirty?

Although the thought experiments above can be helpful in terms of shaking up one of the strongest, long-held beliefs people have—the belief that "I am the voice inside my head"—it's important to go beyond just an intellectual understanding and have a direct experience of this truth.

For many people I've helped with the practice of mindful self-awareness, when they realize intellectually that they are not the voice in their heads, the first question they have is "Who am I then?" But there is no way to answer this question with words or concepts because your true self is beyond thoughts. It is beyond the grasp of the intellect.

Fortunately, just because your true self can't be described or understood with words or concepts, it doesn't mean you can't become intimately familiar with your true self. After all, it's ultimately who you are.

When you practice turning your awareness inward toward the sense of "me" that you're currently experiencing, it's possible for that false sense of self to drop away. In any moment that the ego drops away, the brain has a direct experience of the true self.

When you're being your true self without any identification with the ego, there is an experience of total freedom and perfect peace. This is what is often referred to as an *enlightenment* experience, or *spiritual awakening*.

Many people believe that once you have an experience like this you will never suffer again. In theory, if the experience is deep enough, I believe this could be possible. However, I've never met anyone who was forever free from suffering after one such awakening experience.

In most cases, even if an initial awakening experience is very profound, it's still only the first of many important steps in the process of gradually breaking the habit of identifying with the ego as being the true self. This has been my experience as well.

I'll never forget the first awakening experience in my life. It was a couple of years into my time in prison. After sitting still in mindful self-awareness for twenty minutes or so, I began practicing a contemplation on the death of the body.

There was a point when I visualized the body turning to dust and blowing away in the wind. Because the mind had become very concentrated, there was suddenly an incredible sense of spaciousness. At the same time, there was an incredible surge of energy that was almost overwhelming.

I sat there literally sobbing uncontrollably with tears of ecstatic joy

The Magic of Mindful Self-Awareness

for nearly thirty minutes. It was as though the scars of all the suffering I had ever experienced were healed in an instant. I thought I had entered heaven.

For days after that experience, it seemed like the practice of mindful self-awareness was effortless. Very few thoughts arose and, when they did, they vanished almost immediately without any effort.

There didn't seem to be any trace of the old sense of "me" I had always experienced. There was just "experience happening."

Awareness was no longer trapped inside the head looking out. Although it's hard to put into words, it was as though awareness was both inside looking out and outside looking in. It was something like an "out-of-body" experience, while also feeling more fully in the body than ever before.

This was all a little disorienting at first, but the body and mind were extremely peaceful and happy. Time seemed to no longer exist. Everything was perfect. The world was experienced so vividly, it almost seemed unreal.

After a couple of days, things returned mostly back to "normal." I thought for sure that I was "enlightened" and that I would never suffer again. It wasn't long before I learned that I was not forever free from suffering. I also later learned that the thought "I am enlightened" is a sure sign that there's a lot of ignorance and ego remaining.

Since then, there have been many awakening experiences in my life. It's become easier and easier to allow the old sense of "me," the ego, to drop away on demand, and to experience longer periods of time without recreating that false sense of "me."

I have learned that awakening experiences can be subtle, or very profound, depending on the levels of physical and mental energy present and/or the stability of awareness. I have also learned that it doesn't really matter what the experience is like. What's most important is that we learn how to see through the illusion of the ego, the false sense of self, on a regular basis, and that we create the conditions for stability of awareness.

Every time you see thoughts cease or see through the illusion of the ego, watching the false sense of "me" drop away and experiencing *being* with no false sense of self, wisdom deepens. The more stable awareness is when those insights occur, the deeper the wisdom that is developed. (Again, stable awareness, "concentration," is not effort but an effect of correct practice.)

Each time wisdom deepens, the habitual tendency to identify with the ego or other thoughts becomes a little weaker. Over time, with correct practice, it will become easier and easier to allow the false sense of "me" to drop away and you'll be less likely to identify with it in the first place.

As a result you'll spend increasingly more time free from identification with the ego and other thoughts. You will gradually remove the root cause of suffering and thus become increasingly free from suffering.

Even more important, as you identify with the ego less and less, and are able to more easily drop your identification with this false sense of "me" in cases where you have identified with it, the most important human qualities will be more and more present in your life. As you become less self-centered, and suffer less, you'll find that it becomes easier to be kind, generous, and compassionate. Suffering will gradually be replaced with love, and with the joy that results from extending yourself for the benefit of others.

How to Drop the Habit of Identifying with the Ego

In a general sense, being free from suffering by dropping the habit of identifying with the ego is a function of creating a new habit of turning awareness toward the body and mind as often as needed to wake up to your true self, and then letting go of any mental effort for as long as mindful self-awareness sustains itself.

As the enlightened teacher described in chapter 5, when you sit, know that you are sitting. When you walk, know that you are walking. When you eat, know that you are eating. And so on.

Practicing in this way in daily life will help in the process of gradually dissolving the habit of feeling as though you are the ego. Once the habit of identifying with the ego has sufficiently diminished, you may only need to practice in daily life. However, early on, the habit of identifying with the false sense of "me" will dissolve much faster if you take more time to practice mindful self-awareness while sitting still.

The Magic of Mindful Self-Awareness

This is because when you're sitting still you can truly let go of all mental activity. You don't have to worry about bumping into things, or tripping, or processing much information. You can simply *be*. This helps create the conditions for high levels of both relaxation and stability of awareness.

It is when awareness is stable for long periods of time that deep levels of wisdom can develop. When you clearly see thoughts—especially the sense of being a "me" that seems to be trapped inside your head—cease in the mind, you cultivate the wisdom that sets you free.

This is extremely important. An intellectual understanding that you are not the ego, the current sense of "me" you experience, will do little or nothing to break the habit of identifying with the ego. The only way to break the habit of identifying with the ego and other thoughts is to regularly observe them cease, revealing to you through direct experience that you still exist even when the mind is empty.

To increase the amount of time you practice while sitting still, and thereby more quickly cultivate the wisdom that sets you free, there are a number of options. You could add time for sitting still practice by going to bed just a few minutes earlier, devoting a little more time to sitting before lying down for sleep. You could also get up out of bed a little more quickly when you wake up in the morning.

Also, if you're like most people, you probably spend a good deal of time entertaining yourself with screen time or reading novels. If that's the case, you could trade fifteen to twenty minutes of entertainment time each day for sitting still practice.

At first, just ten additional minutes of sitting still is great. Ideally, you will want to work up to twenty minutes, or more if you like.

Following is a guided practice you could apply while sitting still to clearly see that you're not your thoughts, not the ego, and to thus realize your true self. You could either read this first then do the practice on your own, record yourself reading the practice and then listen to it while sitting still, or visit MattTenney.com to download a recording of me guiding you through the practice.

To start, simply use your inner voice to note what you're doing, "Just sitting."

Then, just be open to whatever you notice.

You don't need to look for anything to notice, just wait and see what arises.

Try to be like a child who has never sat in the place you're sitting now, so you're truly curious.

For now, if you begin thinking about things, just mentally note, "There is thinking happening. That's OK. Now, I'm just sitting."

During this time of sitting still practice, there's nowhere you need to go. There's nothing you need to do.

This is time for just simply sitting and being.

If you persist with just simply sitting with curiosity for a moment or so, you'll almost certainly notice that the body is breathing while it sits.

Each time it breathes in, it expands a little bit, most noticeably in the belly.

Each time it breathes out, it contracts a little bit.

This is not an encouragement to focus on the breath. The breath is just something that can be noticed.

The body is sitting, expanding, and contracting.

The expanding and contracting of the body can be used as a nice timer for your effort to practice mindful self-awareness.

You don't need to practice for some long period of time.

You're simply sitting with curiosity for the duration of just one inhalation.

Then, again, for just one exhalation.

Again, you're not focusing on the breath. You're just sitting, using the expanding and contracting body as a timer.

Continue in this way for ten complete breaths.

Now there is some stability of awareness.

To further stabilize awareness, it can be helpful to sweep through the body with awareness.

You could start with the feet.

With each inhalation, you can notice whatever there is to notice with the feet.

With each exhalation, you can continue noticing sensations while also letting go of any muscles that might be voluntarily contracted in the feet.

Continue for three complete breaths.

Then, continue in the same way with the legs for three complete

The Magic of Mindful Self-Awareness

breaths, then the abdomen, the back, the hands and arms, the neck, and the face and head.

Whenever thoughts arise, you can simply note, "There's thinking about this or that," allow the thoughts to be exactly as they are, and resume noticing what's happening with whatever part of the body you're currently observing.

Once you've spent a few breaths observing the face and head, you could allow awareness to open once again and include the entire body sitting and breathing.

With each inhalation, you can continue noticing whatever there is to notice. With each exhalation, you can continue noticing sensations while also letting go of any muscles that might be voluntarily contracted in the body.

You may notice that along with the objective awareness you have of the body, breathing comes an objective awareness of the mind.

It's very likely that awareness is now stable enough to directly observe thoughts without getting pulled into them.

You may notice that you see thoughts arising and passing away as though you're watching images on a screen.

You may notice that you can hear the inner voice as though you're listening to sounds coming through speakers or earbuds.

It doesn't matter if there are many thoughts, few thoughts, or no thoughts. All that matters is that you continue observing the body sitting, expanding, and contracting.

This provides a foundation for you to see thoughts objectively, without identifying with them.

If you do become entangled with thoughts to the point where you're no longer aware of the expanding and contracting of the body, it's not a problem at all.

This is natural and very likely to occur.

It's also an important part of the practice.

As soon as you notice that you're distracted by thinking, just mentally note, "Oh, I was distracted by thinking. This is not a problem."

Then ask the question, "Is there any thinking now?"

See if you can direct awareness toward the head so that you're both looking at and listening to the place in your head where you think your inner voice is coming from.

You may notice that the mind is completely empty and silent.

At this point, let go of any effort to direct awareness and continue just sitting with curiosity with the next inhalation or exhalation.

There's nothing more to do at this point. You are just simply sitting and doing nothing.

Notice how there are no problems when the mind is empty and silent. There is just peace.

The next time you notice that you're distracted by thinking, just mentally note once again, "Oh, I was distracted by thinking. This is not a problem."

Then ask the question, "Is there any thinking now?"

See if you can direct awareness toward the head so that you're both looking at and listening to the place in your head where you think your inner voice is coming from.

You may notice that the mind is completely empty and silent.

At this point, let go of any effort to direct awareness and continue just sitting with curiosity with the next inhalation or exhalation.

There's nothing more to do at this point. You're just simply sitting and doing nothing.

Notice how there are no problems when the mind is empty and silent. There is just peace.

Continue in this way until the timer sounds.

The Secret to Quickly Developing the Wisdom That Sets You Free

After reading this chapter, a desire to have some type of awakening experience like the one I described may arise. However, the most important thing you can do to realize your true self is to let go of any expectation of anything special happening. In other words, you must be willing to let things be exactly as they are while you are practicing.

It doesn't matter if there's lots of thinking or no thinking. It doesn't matter if thoughts are positive or negative. It doesn't matter if you're experiencing pleasant emotions or unpleasant emotions. The only thing

The Magic of Mindful Self-Awareness

that matters is that you know what's happening and allow whatever arises in your awareness to be exactly as it is.

The moment you wake up to mindful self-awareness in this way, you are already free from suffering. You are already at peace.

At that moment, there is no further effort needed. If you can learn to just appreciate that peace and not expect anything special or magical to happen, you will progress quickly in the practice and both peace and joy will permeate more and more of your formal practice time and more and more of your daily life.

Key Ideas from Chapter 8

1. Pain is an inevitable, objective experience. However, suffering is subjective and optional. It's possible to experience physical and emotional pain without suffering.
2. To be free from suffering, you must remove its root cause: identifying with your current sense of "me," the ego, as being your true self.
3. The practice of mindful self-awareness allows you to gradually break the habit of identifying with the ego and thereby become increasingly free from all suffering.

Action Step from Chapter 8

Please follow the guidance in this chapter to practice sitting still in mindful self-awareness a little more often, and in a way that allows the ego to drop away so you can realize what experience is like without the ego present.

Chapter 9
How to Be Free from Panic Attacks, Anxiety, and Other Unpleasant Emotions

Please take a moment to think of a sound that would be very annoying to you. It could be a song you dislike, fingernails on a chalkboard, or "the most annoying sound in the world" that Jim Carrey made in the classic movie *Dumb and Dumber*. Once you've thought of it, please keep reading.

Now, please imagine that there are very large, powerful speakers, like the type used at a live outdoor concert, blasting the annoying sound you thought of at full volume, to the point where it almost hurts your ears.

How much do you think that would bother you? This experience would probably be unbearable, wouldn't it?

Now imagine that those same speakers were blasting the same sound, at the same volume, but you were 5 kilometers, or 3.2 miles, away from the speakers. How much would the sound bother you then?

At that long distance, the sound probably wouldn't bother you at all, would it? You would probably barely be able to hear it.

The thought experiment above is analogous to two important aspects of the practice of mindful self-awareness.

First, this is very much like what happens as we spend more time being mindfully self-aware instead of being identified with the ego and other thoughts. The ego can be "felt" as a sense of contraction which, for most people, is experienced as being right behind the eyes. Whenever we have unpleasant thoughts, it seems as though they are just one more addition to the sense of contraction. It seems that there's no space around the thoughts or between the thoughts and awareness.

However, the moment you become mindfully self-aware, you'll notice that there is some space between awareness and the thoughts that arise within it. The longer you remain mindfully self-aware, the more space there appears to be around the thoughts, and between thoughts and awareness. The sense of contraction in the head dissipates and there's a sense of greater spaciousness instead.

When there is a lot of space around thoughts, they don't cause suffering, just like the unpleasant sound in the thought experiment above wouldn't cause suffering if there was a lot of space between you and the speakers.

The second way the thought experiment above is analogous to the practice of mindful self-awareness is in terms of how we experience emotions. Over time, with correct practice, it is possible to be free from unpleasant emotions in the same way that it's possible to be free from the unpleasant sound being blasted by the speakers when there's some space between you and the speakers.

Just to be clear, I don't believe it's possible to completely eliminate unpleasant emotions like fear, anger, sadness, or anxiety. Nor do I think that would necessarily be a good thing. These emotions serve a purpose. They are designed to alert the body and mind of potential threats, process a loss, or compel us to change behaviors in ways that protect the body and mind.

However, these emotions are meant to be temporary. They are only meant to be present until their purpose has been served. This is how they work in all the nonhuman animals on the planet.

Imagine a dog that is snarling and barking aggressively at a perceived threat nearby. Within minutes of the threat disappearing from sight and smell, the dog goes back to being happy and playful as if nothing happened.

This is because dogs are almost certainly not thinking about what happened five minutes ago. If they have any thoughts at all, they drop

The Magic of Mindful Self-Awareness

them very quickly. They are not burdened by thoughts of past and future.

But that's not how most humans experience unpleasant emotions is it? For many people, if they become really angry, that anger can last for days, or even years in the form of resentment. This is the result of not being able to let go of thoughts.

I'm confident that as long as you're alive in a human body with a properly functioning nervous system you're going to experience emotional pain. If you lose a loved one, it's going to hurt. However, I also know with certainty that if you accept the emotional pain as a natural part of life you won't add any suffering to the emotional pain, and the emotional pain will pass much more quickly.

In time, with the practice of mindful self-awareness, it's possible to experience unpleasant emotions in the same way that the unpleasant sound would be experienced if the speakers blasting that sound were far away.

You will still experience the emotions, but there will be so much space around them that they will have almost no effect on you. Also, with correct practice, the emotions will start to pass away faster and faster until they only appear as a brief trace that arises and passes away in a matter of minutes or even seconds.

Perhaps most exciting is that, as the wisdom that you are not your ego or other thoughts deepens, the time spent experiencing unpleasant emotions is replaced with either peace or pleasant emotions.

In chapter 3, I wrote that I haven't experienced anxiety or sadness in over ten years, except for a few times for a few brief seconds. Of course, I still get bothered by things. But the experience of being bothered arises and passes within a few seconds.

However, I tear up quite often.

I experience tears of joy, compassion, or inspiration almost every day, sometimes several times a day. Sometimes just looking at my son or daughter triggers these lovely emotions and tears. Sometimes it's witnessing the excellence or creativity of other people. Sometimes it's the beauty of nature.

Often, these pleasant emotions arise for no reason at all other than there has been a sudden or sustained dropping of identification with the ego.

This gradual replacing of unpleasant emotions with pleasant ones is not an experience that is unique to me. This has happened for many thousands of people over the years as a result of breaking the habit of identifying with the ego. And I'm very confident that this will be possible for you if you practice mindful self-awareness frequently and correctly.

How to Be Free from Unpleasant Emotions Quickly, Right Now

Thankfully, while you're patiently waiting for the wisdom to develop that gradually weakens the frequency and duration of unpleasant emotions, it's possible to apply mindful self-awareness right now in a way that will allow you to be free from unpleasant emotions much more quickly. Before exploring that practice, it's important to understand how we get stuck in emotions and how they can spiral out of control.

In a general sense, when you experience something unpleasant, like someone insulting you, an unpleasant emotion—in this case frustration or anger—arises in response to what you experience. An emotion is a physical response in the body. If you're identified with the ego when the unpleasant experience occurs, the corresponding unpleasant physical response (emotion) will be more powerful than necessary.

Also, if you're identified with the ego when the unpleasant experience occurs, you will start having negative thoughts about the experience and/or the emotion that's present. You may start thinking things like *I can't believe he said that to me*, *How dare he*, or *I'll show him he can't just go around insulting people.*

If you've been practicing mindful self-awareness for a while, you may also have thoughts like *I shouldn't be getting so upset. I should be more calm. Why is this bothering me? Am I not practicing correctly?*

Unfortunately, negative thoughts strengthen the physical response in the body. The amygdala, the part of the brain largely responsible for different fight-or-flight-related emotions, tells the body to release more hormones and neurotransmitters that are designed to prepare the body for self-defense.

As the emotion gets stronger, we become less able to see thoughts objectively and the thoughts become stronger, more prevalent, and faster moving. Those thoughts then further fuel the emotional response in the body, which further fuels the thoughts, and so on. This is how emotions like anger and anxiety can quickly spiral out of control and become rage or a panic attack.

The good news is that it's possible to quickly reverse this spiral effect by applying mindful self-awareness to become objectively aware of the emotion and using powerful hacks for stopping the amygdala response.

The moment you begin applying the practice you'll learn in this chapter, the emotion-thought spiral described above begins to unwind. As your emotional state starts to return to normal, thoughts start to slow down and are easier to see objectively.

As the space around thoughts grows, they begin to calm down. This allows the emotional state to return to normal more quickly, which further calms the thoughts, which further calms the emotion, and so on.

Thanks to this powerful practice, strong emotional responses like anger and anxiety, which may currently take hours, or days, or even months to fully subside, can pass within minutes or even seconds.

SCIL: A Powerful Practice for Being Free from Unpleasant Emotions

The SCIL practice for becoming free from unpleasant emotional responses has four steps, which I'll describe below. It is adapted from a practice taught by the well-known monk Thich Nhat Hanh.

S - Stop
C - Control and name
I - Investigate
L - Look for the real cause of the emotion

Step 1 – Stop Interacting with the Perceived Cause of the Emotion

The first step is to stop interacting with the perceived cause of the emotion because this will only add fuel to the proverbial fire. If someone said or did something that contributed to you being angry, you should leave the space that they're in, or at least stop interacting with them. If you're anxious about something, you should stop looking at or listening to anything that reminds you of what you're anxious about.

Step 2 – Control the Breathing and Name the Emotion

The second step of the practice is to consciously control your breathing while naming the emotion that is present.

It was well established decades ago that consciously controlling the activity of breathing, which is normally something the body does all by itself, is a way to "short-circuit" an unpleasant emotional response. The moment you start consciously controlling your breathing, brain activity shifts from the amygdala to the prefrontal cortex, the area of the brain largely responsible for emotional regulation.

In 2007, a neuroscientist at the University of California, Los Angeles named Matthew D. Lieberman first established that using mental noting to name an emotion also decreases activity in the amygdala and shifts activity to the prefrontal cortex. Thus, simply naming an emotion is another way to "short-circuit" an unpleasant emotional response.

By combining the efforts of consciously controlling the breathing and naming the emotion present, you can create a powerful, synergistic effect that helps rapidly de-escalate an unpleasant emotional response. Following is how I recommend applying this.

As soon as you notice you're experiencing an unpleasant emotion, start by slowing down your breathing gradually, focusing on the exhalation. At first, aim to extend your exhalation to two seconds. After each exhalation, simply relax and observe as your body naturally breathes in, allowing the inhalation to be slightly slower than usual. Every few

The Magic of Mindful Self-Awareness

breaths, lengthen the exhalation until it reaches at least five seconds, but ideally seven seconds.

After a couple of rounds of consciously controlling your breathing, you can start to use your inner voice to name the emotion using the following words:

During the inhalation: There is (name the emotion).
During the exhalation: It's OK for (name the emotion) to be present.

I recommend continuing with step 2 until you've had at least ten exhalations that last for at least five seconds (or whatever is the longest time your body will allow), or until you notice a significant reduction in the strength of the emotion.

Step 3 – Investigate Like You're a Scientist in Your Own Body

Note: if at any point you get caught in thinking during this step and the emotion starts to strengthen once again, you can always return to step 2 until you feel ready to practice step 3 once again.

I'll never forget one of the first times I guided someone through step 3 of the SCIL practice. The person was a friend of mine who had been experiencing deep sadness and had been crying for quite a while.

When she reached the point of this step of the practice, her tears had slowed down significantly. However, I noticed that a single tear managed to fall from her eye and slowly run down her cheek.

I asked her, "Can you notice what the tear feels like as it falls down your cheek?"

She noticed. She smiled. Then she started laughing, and the tears of sadness changed to tears of relief and even joy. She was free.

* * *

It's very important that you acknowledge that it's OK for an emotion to be present. Emotions are very natural and important for the survival of the body. Once you acknowledge that it's OK for an emotion to be present, you can shift your response to the emotion.

Instead of either fueling unpleasant emotions, trying to get rid of them or trying to ignore them, you can become curious about your emotions. You can become like a scientist studying your own body. This shift is essential for being free from unpleasant emotions.

You could start by asking the question, *What is this emotion like?*

Then, you can sweep through the body with awareness, as you learned in chapter 8, noticing whatever physical sensation is present in each part, using the breath as a timer. There's no need to control the breathing at this point. Just allow the body to breathe naturally.

You could start with the feet. For three complete breaths or so, just be curious about the feet. With each inhalation, you could notice whatever there is to notice. With each exhalation, you can continue noticing sensations while also letting go of any muscles that might be voluntarily contracted in the feet.

You can then continue in the same way with the legs, the abdomen, the back, the hands and arms, the neck, and the face and head.

Whenever thoughts arise, you can simply note, *There's thinking about this or that,* allow the thoughts to be exactly as they are, and resume noticing what's happening with whatever part of the body you're currently observing.

Once you've spent a few breaths observing the face and head, you could allow awareness to open once again and include the entire body sitting and breathing.

With each inhalation, you can continue noticing whatever there is to notice. With each exhalation, you can continue noticing sensations while also letting go of any muscles that might be voluntarily contracted in the body.

By observing the emotion objectively in this way, you make the shift to mindful self-awareness and are thus no longer identified with thoughts. They just arise and pass away without pulling you into a discussion with yourself.

When you're no longer identified with thoughts, the fuel for the emotion is removed. You're no longer perpetuating the problem, and the resulting emotion, with your thoughts. You can simply drop the problem.

If there's no problem, the body doesn't feel threatened so your emotional state returns to normal.

Step 4: Look for the Real Cause of the Emotion

You may have noticed that in step 1, I use the language "the perceived cause of the emotion" and "a person who contributed to an emotion." This is intentional.

If you really reflect on what causes an emotion, it's actually the perception we have of an experience, not the experience itself. For instance, if you're out walking at night and see a snake on the path, the emotion of fear will probably arise. Again, this is a natural response that is helpful for protecting the body.

However, what would happen if you shined a flashlight on the snake and realized that it wasn't a snake at all but a section of rope that was coiled up and looked like a snake? The emotion of fear in your body would immediately start fading away and the emotional state in your body would quickly return to normal.

This is how all emotions arise. As you read in chapter 8, if you want an event to happen, there's no problem. Unpleasant emotions only arise when we attach to a desire to get something we want or to a desire to get rid of something we don't want.

By practicing mindful self-awareness and more regularly realizing your true self, you will gradually change the initial response you have to events. It's quite possible that you could reach a point where next to nothing bothers you because your initial response to all experiences is to be OK with whatever is happening.

However, that takes time, and you have no direct control over when wisdom will develop. Thus, aiming for the ideal of almost never having an unpleasant emotional response will actually slow your progress. It's very important to acknowledge and accept whatever emotional response arises in your body at any given moment. This is one reason why the first three steps in SCIL are important.

Where you do have some control, and the best place to focus your efforts early on in the practice, is the degree to which you perpetuate unpleasant emotional responses with your thinking. By following the first three steps of the SCIL practice, you can learn in a relatively short amount of time how to let go of identification with your thinking and thus stop creating and perpetuating the problem.

The fourth step in the SCIL practice can help with both the initial emotional response and the degree to which you perpetuate unpleasant emotions. This step is to look for the real cause of the emotion.

As you read above, your perception of an experience is the real cause of any initial unpleasant emotional response and for the perpetuation of any unpleasant emotion. If you perceive a snake on the path, you'll experience fear. If you perceive a rope on the path instead, you will not experience fear.

It's very important that you don't try to skip right to this step of the SCIL practice. As you read in chapter 4, if you just try to tell yourself better stories, without allowing thoughts and emotions to be seen objectively, you'll likely do more harm than good. Also, you'll be missing out on priceless opportunities to develop the wisdom that your true self is not the ego or other thoughts and emotions.

That being said, once you've taken time to be fully present with an unpleasant emotion and allowed it to unwind using the first three steps of the SCIL practice, there is tremendous value in taking time to question the stories you tell yourself.

You could start by simply asking the question, *What story was I telling myself while that unpleasant emotion was present?* Then take some time to honestly reflect on how you perceived the experience.

Once you're clear on what story you were telling yourself, you could then ask yourself, *Is there another story that could explain what happened equally as well?*

For instance, imagine someone cut you off on the highway. You might have initially told yourself that the person in the other car intentionally cut you off because they are selfish and inconsiderate. Could it also be true that the person was rushing to get to the hospital to see a critically injured loved one before she died?

Maybe someone is routinely unkind to you. Perhaps you've been telling yourself that he is a bad person. Could it also be true that although this person wants nothing more than to be kind, he was abused as a child, both emotionally and physically, and thus learned unskillful behaviors in childhood from which he struggles to break free?

Maybe there's something you're very anxious about, like a job interview or tough conversation. Perhaps you've been telling yourself how badly this could go and all the negative consequences that could result from it going badly. Could it also be true that the experience could go very well or, if it doesn't go well, that the consequences won't be nearly as bad as you've been thinking?

Transforming Unpleasant Emotions Into the Most Pleasant Emotion of All

In many cases, you'll need to come up with hypothetical alternative stories to tell yourself about an event or experience. However, in some cases, you'll be able to ask people questions about what's going on for them. And, when you do, you will almost certainly understand them better.

You'll also see more clearly that people are just doing the best they can with what they've got. In any moment that people are identified with the ego, they are victims of how they've been programmed by their genetics and life experiences up to this moment in time. Without mindful self-awareness, people can only do what they've been programmed to do.

When you understand this simple truth, or you understand what might have directly led to the actions of another person contributing to an unpleasant emotion for you, whatever elements of the emotion that still remain at this point are replaced by the most pleasant emotion of all: compassion.

Compassion is the aspiration to help relieve suffering. It is so pleasant that the first time you experience the shift from an unpleasant emotion to compassion, you may be overwhelmed with joy.

By applying the SCIL practice to transform unpleasant emotions into compassion, you'll actually learn to welcome unpleasant experiences and emotions as opportunities to deepen your compassion for others and for yourself. This is one of the most powerful ways the practice of mindful self-awareness can help you live a life that is almost entirely free of suffering and that is also deeply meaningful and fulfilling.

The Magic of Mindful Self-Awareness

Key Ideas from Chapter 9

1. Although emotions are important, and you'll probably never completely eliminate unpleasant emotions, it's possible to dramatically reduce the frequency of unpleasant emotions and the amount of time it takes to recover from an unpleasant emotion using the SCIL practice.
2. The SCIL practice consists of four steps:
    - S - Stop interacting with the perceived cause of the emotion
    - C - Control the breathing and name the emotion
    - I - Investigate like you're a scientist in your own body
    - L - Look for the real cause of the emotion

Action Steps from Chapter 9

1. Please take a few moments to do the SCIL practice a few times, if you haven't already done so, so that you have a little practice with it before you actually need it. You can simulate an emotional response by doing some jumping jacks or other form of exercise that gets your heart rate and breathing up. Then, you could use the SCIL practice to calm the body and mind.
2. Please create a calendar event or an alarm on your phone that reminds you to do the SCIL practice a couple of times, one day each week, until you feel very confident you'll be able to apply it when you need it.

Chapter 10
A Simple Path to Living a Deeply Meaningful Life

There's a story about a chief named Bakari of an ancient tribe in what is now Kenya. Chief Bakari aspired to be the most effective ruler possible. It occurred to him one day that if he knew the answers to three questions he would certainly be a great leader. The three questions were as follows:

What is the most important time to do each thing?
Who is the most important person to work with?
What is the most important task to pursue?

Chief Bakari became very excited about the possibility of learning the answers to the three questions. He asked the other tribal leaders to send a message across the land stating that anyone who could answer the three questions satisfactorily would be given the largest group of cattle anyone had ever seen. This would be the equivalent of over a million US dollars in today's currency.

Because of the promise of such wealth, many people came from far-off places with their answers to the questions.

In response to the first question, some people said that the chief should create a calendar that would allow him to plan out every minute of every day of the year so he would always get things done on time. Others said that he should build a council of wise elders he could consult every time he wanted to know when the best time was to do each task.

Bakari wasn't happy with any of the answers to the first question.

In response to the second question, some people said that the most important task was to develop knowledge. Others said it was to build wealth. Others said it was to develop great warriors.

Again, Bakari was not satisfied with any of the answers.

In response to the third question, people gave a variety of answers that included working with warriors, working with cattle breeders, and working with religious leaders.

Bakari did not think any of the answers were correct.

The chief was just about to give up on his quest to find the answers to the three questions when an idea came to him. He remembered that there was a spiritual elder who lived nearby in solitude near the top of a mountain.

Many people claimed that the hermit was the wisest person anyone had ever met. *Surely*, Bakari thought, *if anyone could answer my three questions, it would be this wise old hermit.*

Bakari decided to go visit the hermit, but he was warned that the spiritual elder was very wary of people with wealth and power. He would never see a wealthy chief. So Bakari decided to disguise himself as a peasant in order to have a chance of being received by the hermit.

After walking half a day with two of his best warriors, Bakari arrived at the mountain. He walked about a third of the way up the mountain and left the two warriors to finish the hike alone.

When Bakari arrived at the hermit's home, he found the wise elder cultivating the soil with a digging tool, preparing it for planting seeds.

Bakari said, "Hello, wise elder."

The hermit looked at him with a warm smile and continued digging.

Chief Bakari said, "Dear elder, I am told that you are very wise and I believe that you could help me answer three questions that are very important to me. The questions are:

What is the most important time to do each thing?

Who is the most important person to work with?

What is the most important task to pursue?"

The hermit smiled and nodded at Bakari and went right back to digging. The work was clearly challenging for the hermit because of his age. He grunted loudly every time he dug with the tool.

Bakari said, "That looks tiring. May I help you with the digging?"

The hermit smiled warmly and handed Chief Bakari the tool.

Bakari dug one row, and then another. After nearly fifteen minutes of digging, Bakari remembered that he had come to get answers to his three questions, and said, "I almost forgot. I was hoping you could answer three questions that are very important to me. The questions are:

What is the most important time to do each thing?

Who is the most important person to work with?

What is the most important task to pursue? Are you able to help?"

The hermit replied, "I feel rested. Thank you for your help. I can continue digging now."

Bakari said, "No. That's quite alright. I'm happy to help you dig."

He went right back to digging. This time, nearly an hour passed before he remembered why he had come.

Bakari said, "Dear wise elder, it is getting late and I will need to head home soon. Before I go, I would be very grateful if you could answer my three questions. Are you able to help?"

At that moment, the hermit pointed to the tree line. A bearded man with a spear was running right toward Bakari, holding his hand over his stomach.

Just before reaching Bakari, the man fell down and passed out. His hand moved away from his stomach, revealing a bloody gash.

Chief Bakari immediately took a piece of cloth and used it to try to stop the bleeding. The blood quickly soaked the cloth, so Bakari ran to a nearby creek to rinse it out and then came back again to put pressure on the wound. After rinsing the cloth several times, the bleeding finally stopped.

A few minutes later, the bearded man regained consciousness. He quietly whispered, "I'm very thirsty."

The Magic of Mindful Self-Awareness

Bakari asked the hermit for a cup and ran to get water from the hermit's water supply. He brought the water to the bearded man, who took a few drinks and then fell asleep.

At this point, it was almost dark. Bakari carried the man to the hermit's hut and laid him on a sleeping mat. Bakari sat down and leaned against the doorway to the hut. He was so tired that he fell asleep after just a few minutes.

In the morning, Bakari woke up just as the sun was rising. A little confused, he looked around. He tried to remember why he was sitting in the doorway of the hut. When he looked in the direction of the bearded man, he made eye contact with the man.

The bearded man said, "I am so sorry. Please forgive me."

Bakari replied, "What have you done that I should forgive?"

The bearded man said, "You do not know me, Chief Bakari, but I know you. In the last war between our tribes your warriors severely injured my brother and you ordered that all my cattle be taken from me and given to your tribe. I vowed that I would get my revenge.

"I have been spying on you for weeks now. When I saw you leave your warriors on the mountain, I realized I would never have a better opportunity to hunt you down. I climbed a little higher up the mountain and waited to ambush you when you returned.

"But you were gone so long. I became impatient and decided to leave my hiding place. When I did, your warriors, who had changed their position, saw me. I was able to outrun them and lose them, but I accidentally ran into a sharp stick that punctured my belly.

"I did not give up, though. When I finally saw you I thought for sure I would get my revenge. So, there I was running at you with the intention of hurting you, and you responded by saving my life.

"I am both ashamed and deeply grateful to you. I vow that I will be your servant for as long as I live."

Chief Bakari was so happy that he was able to reconcile with a former enemy. He replied, "My friend, that is not necessary at all. In fact, I will make sure that you receive the best care for your wound from my medicine men. Also, I will make sure that all your cattle are returned to you."

Bakari went to summon his warriors and asked them to carry the bearded man back to the village and have his wound treated.

Dwelling in compassion, he felt so happy that he almost forgot why he had come to see the hermit. He suddenly remembered when he heard the wise elder working in the garden near the hut.

Chief Bakari found the hermit planting seeds in the soil they had cultivated the day before. He said, "Good morning, wise elder."

Knowing exactly what Bakari was going to say, the hermit looked at him with a warm smile and said, "If you look closely, you'll see that your three questions have already been answered."

Confused, Bakari replied, "What do you mean?"

"Yesterday," the hermit replied, "the time you spent helping me dig in the garden was the most important time. Had you not done that, it's very likely that you would have walked down the mountain and been killed by the bearded man.

"Likewise, the most important person to work with was me, and the most important task was to help me dig.

"Later," the hermit continued, "the most important time was the time you spent treating the bearded man's wound and getting him water. Had you not done that, you might have never experienced the joy of reconciliation.

"The most important person was the bearded man. The most important task was to help him.

"Chief Bakari, the most important time is always the present moment. That is the only time over which you have any control.

"The most important person is always the person you are with in the present moment. You have no idea if you'll ever interact with another person in the future.

"The most important task is to help the person you are with to be happy. That, Chief Bakari, is ultimately the only pursuit in life that truly matters."

* * *

Often, when people first learn that the cause of suffering is attachment to desires, and ultimately attachment to the false sense of "me" as being

The Magic of Mindful Self-Awareness

our true self, some natural concerns arise. People wonder if they'll become detached from life, or if they'll lose their drive for achievement.

If you're having thoughts like this, please do not worry. This is quite normal.

These thoughts are primarily a result of the ego feeling threatened. When the ego feels threatened, it creates all sorts of thoughts to defend itself.

However, the practice of mindful self-awareness will not cause you to become detached from life, and it will not cause you to lose your drive for achievement. In fact, if you practice mindful self-awareness correctly, you will feel more connected to life than ever before, and you will tap into incredible energy for achievement.

From the point of view of the intellect, spending as much time as possible being aware of your body and mind—instead of being identified with your ego and other thoughts—sounds like you're just passively watching life happen. But that's not what the actual experience is like.

You experience the world through your nervous system. As long as that nervous system is functioning properly, you're going to continue experiencing all the sights, sounds, smells, tastes, and physical sensations that are part of the miracle of being alive in a human body.

In fact, you'll be able to more fully enjoy them because you'll be less distracted by thinking.

Even more importantly, each time the brain has direct experience of being aware without being identified with the ego, it is less likely to be a reflection of the ego, which is never satisfied, inherently selfish, and always slightly afraid of dying. Instead, the brain and the personality it creates become a reflection of your true self.

Since your true self is always at peace, never suffers, and is completely satisfied and fulfilled at all times, every moment spent being your true self helps the brain and the personality it creates to reflect peace, happiness, and fulfillment.

Again, this is not something you should just "believe" or "not believe." You can, and should, go verify this with your own experience.

How Fulfillment Boosts Achievement Drive and Impact

In addition to helping you be happier and more fulfilled, the practice also helps with achievement, and particularly the impact you make in the world. Something interesting happens to achievement drive when you're completely fulfilled. Although the drive to achieve doesn't go away, it changes.

Instead of doing things in life as a means to achieve some goal, we do them *just to do them*. We don't clean the dishes to get clean dishes. We do it just to enjoy the miracle of being alive in a human body that is able to clean dishes.

We don't exercise to lose weight. We do it just to enjoy the miracle of being alive in a human body that is able to exercise.

We don't work to make money. We do it just to enjoy the miracle of being alive in a human body that is able to work.

If you reflect on this, you'll realize that living this way will make you much more effective at whatever you do, and even more likely to achieve your goals.

Let's consider driving as a simple example. Are you more likely to safely reach your destination if you are fully present for the act of driving a car, or if you're constantly staring at the destination on a map?

If you're trying to get a promotion at work, are you more likely to get promoted if you're constantly thinking about what life will be like when you're promoted, or if you're fully present with the job you have now and do the best you can at that job?

If you're trying to get physically stronger, will you be more successful if you're constantly thinking about your end goal or if you're fully present for each repetition of the weights you lift?

Although everyone I've ever asked about this agrees that the best way to achieve goals is to be fully present during the activities that will help you reach your goals, some people worry that if they're completely satisfied and fulfilled, they won't set goals in the first place. They worry that they'll lose all ambition.

For people who practice correctly, though, what happens is the exact opposite.

Big Goals Are More Fulfilling than Small Goals

With consistent practice of mindful self-awareness, even if you don't necessarily go looking for problems to solve, you're much more likely to notice problems to solve in your everyday life because you're much more present.

Also, because you're not so attached to your own short-term desires, you're much more likely to be willing to, and even excited about, solving the problems you encounter in your daily life.

In fact, you may find that you set bigger goals than ever related to solving problems you see. This has certainly been the case for me.

When I first realized that I could make an impact on the entire world by focusing on helping the people right around me, I decided to set a very big goal for my life. In my lifetime, I want to create the conditions for a permanent end to poverty, violence, and other unnecessary suffering in our world. I'm not sure there could be a bigger goal than that.

Although I take my life goal very seriously, and devote all my work toward achieving it, I'm not attached to it at all. Whether I achieve it or not has no effect on my fulfillment in life.

I break this big life goal down into daily and momentary goals that allow me to see frequent progress.

My daily goal is to leave each person and place a little better off than I find them. In each moment, I try to remember to be mindfully self-aware so that I am better able to achieve my daily goal. I frequently reflect on whether I've improved at this recently. Seeing frequent progress further adds to the joy I experience in life.

Also, my big life goal forces me to set other big goals related to my work. But I don't set those goals out of a feeling of obligation or attachment. I set those goals because there's no reason not to! Why not do awesome things during the short time we have being alive on earth as humans?

I find that bigger goals are much more useful than small ones because big goals force us to grow. We can't achieve big goals doing what we've always done. Since growth is one of the core needs humans have for thriving, big goals contribute significantly to thriving.

Interestingly, another benefit of the practice of mindful self-awareness is that it helps remove one of the primary blocks for setting and achieving big goals.

First, the blocks for noticing and responding to problems you encounter are removed because you're more present and less selfish. Also, the blocks for most effectively solving those problems are largely removed because you're not attached to the outcome and are better able to focus on the task at hand.

Additionally, the practice of mindful self-awareness helps remove the biggest block to setting and achieving big goals: the belief that you can't do something.

With correct practice, you're able to let go of limiting thoughts and beliefs. You let go of any past identity as being "you," and instead operate from the wisdom that who you are as a person is not fixed. You are constantly evolving. You can be whoever you want to be.

With correct regular practice, you're more likely to live from the wisdom that who you are in this moment is not who you'll be tomorrow. When contemplating a big goal, instead of thinking, *I can't do this*, you think, *Who would I have to become to achieve this?*

Each Moment of Life Can Be Deeply Meaningful, Regardless of Your Situation in Life

As exciting as all of this is, it's important to remember that thinking will not make any of this real for you. Only taking action will make this real for you.

In the story you read at the beginning of this chapter—which was originally told by Leo Tolstoy and I modified for this book—you were reminded of three, extremely powerful truths. Somewhere deep inside, you already know these truths:

The most important time is always the present moment. That is the only time over which you have any control.

The most important person is always the person you are with in the present moment. You have no idea if you'll ever interact with another person in the future.

The Magic of Mindful Self-Awareness

The most important task is to help the person you are with to be happy. Ultimately, that is the only pursuit in life that truly matters.

Fortunately, these truths don't have to remain as just inspiring words that you read in a book. These truths can become your living reality every day.

In any moment that you remember to become mindfully self-aware, you are not identified with or distracted by your thoughts. You are fully present with what you're doing now and who you're with. This alone helps you to live the three truths above.

Also, because you're not identified with the ego, your natural response is to leave each person and place a little better off than you found them, even if that means just being a peaceful, kind person when those around you are not at peace or not being kind.

In any moment that you're mindfully self-aware, you make a positive impact on others just by being alive.

This means that you can live a happy, meaningful life right now, wherever you are and whatever your situation is in life. It's possible to realize deep meaning and fulfillment in each and every moment of your life.

This is the true magic of mindful self-awareness.

* * *

Before you stop reading and go on to the next activity, I'd like to give you an opportunity to help others right now.

If you found this book helpful, and think it will be helpful to others, there's an easy way for you to help other people find the book.

If you haven't done so already, please leave an honest review of this book on Amazon.com that includes at least a couple of sentences sharing your thoughts on the book.

There's a QR code linking to the Amazon.com review section below.

Please scan the code with the camera on your phone, tap the link that appears on your phone, and take 60 seconds to leave your review.

Every review—including yours—makes an impact by helping more people find the book on Amazon.com.

I would personally be very grateful to you for leaving an honest review.

More importantly, other people will be thankful to you because you will have helped them discover a book that could significantly change their lives for the better.

Thank you in advance, my friend!

Please Scan Me to Leave a Review

The Magic of Mindful Self-Awareness

Key Ideas from Chapter 10

1. The practice of mindful self-awareness helps you set and achieve big goals by being more present during the most important activities for achieving those goals and freeing yourself from limiting thought patterns and beliefs.
2. Big goals lead to more fulfillment than small ones because they force you to grow. Growth is a core need for thriving.
3. The most important time is always the present moment. That is the only time over which you have any control.
4. The most important person is always the person you are with in the present moment.
5. The most important task is to help the person you are with to be happy. Ultimately, that is the only pursuit in life that truly matters.

Action Step for Chapter 10

You may have noticed that the three truths from this chapter are included on *The Magic of Mindful Self-Awareness Practice Tracker*. Please make a commitment to read these three truths every morning for the next thirty days.

An Additional Resource

There is a companion YouTube channel called *The Magic of Mindful Self-Awareness*.

This channel has videos to further help you with the practice. I intend to post more videos that are responses to questions from subscribers.

If you have a question about the practice of mindful self-awareness, please subscribe to the channel and leave your question as a comment in one of the videos. I'll do my best to answer your question or one like it.

Acknowledgments

There are so many people I'd like to thank for contributing to this book. In a way, everyone has contributed to it in some way or another.

In the interest of saving paper, I'm going to focus on people who have most directly contributed to this book.

First, I'd like to thank my wife, Leah. In addition to being a wonderful life partner, she is a highly accomplished writer and editor. She was the first person to read the manuscript for this book and offered many extremely helpful suggestions that made this book much better than it would have been without her help.

I'd like to thank Muriel Call, Grisel Marsh, and Emma Moylan for the great work they did copyediting and proofreading the manuscript for this book.

I'd also like to thank my literary agent, Michael Palgon, who also offered helpful suggestions for making this book better. Notably, he did this despite the fact that we decided to independently publish this book before considering selling it to a major publisher. Thus, Michael, who is a true mensch, took considerable time to help with this book despite having no guarantee that he would ever benefit from it financially.

I'd like to thank Michael Carroll, who is one of the wisest people I have ever met. I consider him a teacher of mine, whether he agrees or not. He also offered some very helpful suggestions for improving this book.

I'd like to thank Jon Gordon, who introduced me to Matt Holt when Matt was a VP at Wiley. Without Jon's help, there's a good chance I might have never been published by a major publisher. Jon sees the power, as I do, of helping people who help others, as this is a highly leveraged way of making a positive impact in the world.

I'd like to thank Matt Holt as well. Matt is a good friend and my favorite publisher. Matt published *Inspire Greatness* in 2024. When I told him of my plans to initially publish this book independently, he fully supported me. In fact, he offered helpful suggestions despite having no guarantee that he would ever publish this book. This is Matt's way. He adds a lot of value in the lives of others with no expectation of getting anything in return. I believe this largely explains why Matt is so successful.

I'd like to thank all the monks and nuns around the world, from all the different spiritual traditions, who help ensure spiritual practices are grounded not just in theories and beliefs but in the wisdom that arises from consistent, lifelong practice.

Finally, I'd like to thank you. If you're reading these acknowledgments, there's a good chance that you have read this entire book, and that you're going to develop habits that benefit you and everyone around you. Your efforts truly could change the world.

About the Author

Matt Tenney envisions a world in which all leaders and workplace cultures consistently make a positive impact on the well-being and growth of team members. He believes this would create the conditions for a permanent end to poverty, violence, and other unnecessary suffering.

Since 2002, Matt has helped thousands of people to apply mindful self-awareness to be happier, less stressed, and more effective. He has also helped hundreds of clients—including many Fortune 500 companies—to develop highly effective leaders who improve employee engagement, performance, and retention through his books, consulting work, and via the groundbreaking leadership development and employee engagement platform offered by his company, PeopleThriver.

Matt is frequently invited to deliver keynote speeches at company leadership meetings, events for state and national associations, and large conferences. He is known for giving inspiring keynotes that keep audiences fully engaged and provide powerful insights and tools for being a great leader and living a happier and more fulfilling life.

When he's not traveling for speaking engagements, Matt can be found in Nashville, Tennessee.

Notes

1. Strictly speaking, the term *mindful self-awareness* is redundant with *mindfulness*. I use the term *mindful self-awareness* to describe the practice you'll learn in this book for two reasons. First, the term *mindfulness* has become so ubiquitous as to become essentially meaningless. Its use has grown to describe everything from meditation to playing tennis to taking a nap. Second, I want to highlight what I believe is the most important aspect of mindfulness practice: being aware of the mind and body and thoughts instead of being identified with them. It is this awareness of the body, mind, and thoughts, that allows us to be effortlessly and fully present with experience.
2. A Systematic Review and Meta-analysis of the Effects of Meditation on Empathy, Compassion, and Prosocial Behaviors. "The results of several systematic reviews and meta-analyses of mindfulness-based interventions suggest that these treatments significantly improve stress, anxiety, depression, quality of life, and emotion regulation across a range of psychiatric and medical populations (Bohlmeijer, Prenger, Taal, & Cuijpers, 2010." https://pmc.ncbi.nlm.nih.gov/articles/PMC6081743/#R5.
3. A wandering mind is an unhappy mind. https://pubmed.ncbi.nlm.nih.gov/21071660/.
4. American Adults Express Increasing Anxiousness in Annual Poll; Stress and Sleep are Key Factors Impacting Mental Health. https://www.psychiatry.org/news-room/news-releases/annual-poll-adults-express-increasing-anxiousness.